The College Affordability Crisis

Recent Titles in
21st-Century Turning Points

The #MeToo Movement
Laurie Collier Hillstrom

The NFL National Anthem Protests
Margaret Haerens

School Shootings and the Never Again Movement
Laurie Collier Hillstrom

The Vaping Controversy
Laurie Collier Hillstrom

Family Separation and the U.S.–Mexico Border Crisis
Laurie Collier Hillstrom

The College Affordability Crisis

Laurie Collier Hillstrom

21st-Century Turning Points

 ABC-CLIO®

An Imprint of ABC-CLIO, LLC
Santa Barbara, California • Denver, Colorado

Library of Congress Cataloging in Publication Control Number: 2020912843

ISBN: 978–1–4408–7723–0 (print)
    978–1–4408–7724–7 (ebook)

24 23 22 21 20   1 2 3 4 5

This book is also available as an eBook.

ABC-CLIO
An Imprint of ABC-CLIO, LLC

ABC-CLIO, LLC
147 Castilian Drive
Santa Barbara, California 93117
www.abc-clio.com

This book is printed on acid-free paper ∞
Manufactured in the United States of America

Contents

Series Foreword   vii

Chapter 1   **Overview of the College Affordability Crisis**   1

Chapter 2   **Landmark Events**   11
History of Higher Education in the United States
    (1636-1980s)   11
A Sociologist Questions the Value of Higher Education
    (1979)   16
Escalation in College Costs (1980s-2000s)   20
Sallie Mae and the Student Debt Crisis (1972-2019)   27
The Public Service Loan Forgiveness Program (2007)   34
For-Profit College Scams (2008-2018)   40
The Occupy Colleges Movement (2011)   47
The "Operation Varsity Blues" College Admissions
    Scandal (2019)   50

Chapter 3   **Impacts of the College Affordability Crisis**   59
College Affordability and Income Inequality   59
Hunger and Homelessness among College Students   68
Proposals for Tuition-Free College   75
Student Loan Debt and the U.S. Economy   81
Student Loan Debt and Individual Borrowers   87
Proposals for Student Loan Forgiveness   95

Chapter 4   **Profiles**   101
F. King Alexander (1963-)
    University administrator and advocate of public funding
    for higher education   101

Bryan Caplan (1971-)
  *Economist who proposed eliminating government subsidies
  for higher education*   105
Alan Collinge (1970-)
  *Consumer protection advocate and founder of Student
  Loan Justice*   109
Randall Collins (1941-)
  *Sociologist who raised questions about the value of
  higher education*   112
Betsy DeVos (1958-)
  *Private school advocate and secretary of education in
  the Trump administration*   115
Seth Frotman (1978?-)
  *Former student loan ombudsman for the Consumer
  Financial Protection Bureau*   119
Betsy Mayotte (1973?-)
  *Borrowers' rights advocate and founder of the Institute
  of Student Loan Advisors*   122
Elizabeth Warren (1949-)
  *U.S. senator who promoted tuition-free public college
  and student debt forgiveness*   124

Further Resources   129

Index   139

Series Foreword

21st-Century Turning Points is a general reference series that has been crafted for use by high school and undergraduate students as well as members of the general public. The purpose of the series is to give readers a clear, authoritative, and unbiased understanding of major fast-breaking events, movements, people, and issues that are transforming American life, culture, and politics in this turbulent new century. Each volume constitutes a one-stop resource for learning about a single issue or event currently dominating America's news headlines and political discussions—issues or events that, in many cases, are also driving national debate about our country's leaders, institutions, values, and priorities.

Each volume in the *21st-Century Turning Points* series begins with an **Overview** of the event or issue that is the subject of the book. It then provides a suite of informative chronologically arranged narrative entries on specific **Landmarks** in the evolution of the event or issue in question. This section provides both vital historical context and insights into present-day news events to give readers a full and clear understanding of how current issues and controversies evolved.

The next section of the book is devoted to examining the **Impacts** of the event or issue in question on various aspects of American life, including political, economic, cultural, and interpersonal implications. It is followed by a chapter of biographical **Profiles** that summarize the life experiences and personal beliefs of prominent individuals associated with the event or issue in question.

Finally, each book concludes with a topically organized **Further Resources** list of important and informative resources—from influential books to fascinating websites—to which readers can turn for additional information, and a carefully compiled subject **Index**.

These complementary elements, found in every book in the series, work together to create an evenhanded, authoritative, and user-friendly tool for gaining a deeper and more accurate understanding of the fast-changing nation in which we live—and the issues and moments that define us as we move deeper into the twenty-first century.

CHAPTER ONE

Overview of the College Affordability Crisis

Millions of Americans view higher education as an essential step on the path toward economic prosperity and social advancement. The idea that anyone can succeed through hard work and education is deeply ingrained in the national psyche. "When we open the doors to college, we open the doors to opportunity," said former president Bill Clinton. "When we make college more affordable, we make the American Dream more achievable" (Clinton 2000).

Research corroborates the socioeconomic value of higher education. People who complete a bachelor's degree, for instance, can expect to earn $1 million more in lifetime income than people whose education ends with high school. Studies also find greater levels of career stability, job satisfaction, homeownership, and even health and longevity among college graduates. Some advocates assert that higher education opens minds, challenges perspectives, and imparts a broader understanding of the world, thus benefitting society through informed debate and increased civic engagement. Other supporters argue that an educated workforce promotes economic growth and helps the United States remain competitive in a technology-driven global business environment. For these reasons, generations of Americans have considered the cost of college to be a worthwhile investment.

Beginning with the passage of the Higher Education Act (HEA) of 1965, the federal government established a system of grants, loans, and outreach programs intended to make college more affordable for high-achieving students of limited means. "This act means the path of knowledge is open to all that have the determination to walk it," President Lyndon B. Johnson said at the signing ceremony. "It means that a high school senior anywhere in this great land of ours can apply to any college or any university in any of the 50 states and not be turned away because his family is poor" (Johnson 1965). The federal commitment to subsidizing the cost of college for low-income students reflected the widespread view that higher education produces benefits to American society as well as to individual citizens.

In the twenty-first century, however, escalating tuition costs have made college unaffordable for many students and raised questions about the value of higher education. Beginning in the 1980s—around the time the tail end of the postwar baby-boom generation reached college age—the cost of higher education grew three to four times faster than the overall rate of inflation in the U.S. economy. As a result, the average cost to earn a four-year degree at colleges and universities nationwide increased by more than 1,100 percent in 35 years (Connell 2016, xiv). Since median annual wages remained stagnant during this period, a year of college that accounted for 22 percent of an average family's annual income in 1989 required 45 percent of that family's yearly income in 2016 (Selingo 2016). "As Americans, we believe in educational access and opportunity for all," said higher education administrator F. King Alexander. "But more than 200 universities charge the equivalent of the median American annual household income—$51,000 —or more. We are pricing our students out of their futures" (Alexander 2016).

Rising College Costs

The parents of today's college students often scraped together enough money to cover their tuition by working at summer jobs. One study found that baby boomers who earned bachelor's degrees in 1976 had to work approximately 300 hours—or around eight months of full-time employment—at the prevailing minimum wage to pay for four years of tuition at a public college. In contrast, members of the millennial generation (people born between 1981 and 1996) had to work nearly 4,500 hours—or more than two years at a full-time minimum-wage job—to afford a four-year public-college degree in 2006 (Hoffower 2019). By 2019, average annual tuition and fees for in-state students at public universities exceeded $10,000, while the average annual tuition at private colleges approached $37,000 (Powell and Kerr 2019). After factoring in the cost of food, housing, books, supplies, transportation, and other expenses, the full cost of attendance spiraled much higher. One analyst estimated that it would take a student 9,700 hours, or nearly five years of full-time minimum-wage work, to pay for a four-year degree from a public college in 2019 (Watson 2019).

Economists, policymakers, and university administrators offer many different explanations for skyrocketing college prices. Some attribute rising tuition rates to an increase in demand for higher education, as more employers require at least a bachelor's degree for entry-level jobs. According to the National Center for Education Statistics (2020), between 2000 and 2018 U.S. undergraduate enrollment increased by 26 percent, from 13.2 million students to 16.6 million students. The college enrollment rate for Americans between the ages of 18 and 24 grew from 35 percent to 41 percent during this period. Many institutions constructed facilities, expanded programs, and hired staff to accommodate additional students.

Other analysts blame rising tuition rates at the nation's 1,600 public colleges and universities on reductions in state funding for higher education. States responded to declining tax revenues following the 2008 recession by cutting more than $7 billion from their higher education budgets over the next decade (Johnson 2019). Many universities made up for the state disinvestment by passing a larger share of instructional costs along to students in the form of tuition increases. On the other hand, some analysts attribute rising college costs to the increased availability of federal student aid—especially in the form of government-subsidized education loans. Colleges and universities no longer found it necessary to keep tuition rates low, according to critics, when students could easily borrow money to cover the higher costs.

Some critics contend that out-of-control spending at colleges is a major factor in rising tuition costs. They point to multi-million-dollar salaries for university presidents and football coaches, significant increases in the size of administrative staffs, and the proliferation of such campus amenities as gourmet dining facilities, plush residence halls, and fancy student fitness centers as examples of noneducational expenses that get passed along to students.

Other analysts blame college rankings, such as those published annually by *U.S. News and World Report,* for soaring tuition prices. Most high-profile ranking systems reward schools on the basis of reputation, selectivity, and per-student spending, rather than on measures of affordability or access. Critics claim that these rankings give college administrators powerful incentives to spend money in an effort to maximize the institution's prestige and attract more students. "I think *U.S. News* has done more damage to the higher education marketplace than any single enterprise that's out there," said Alexander. "We're spending more money on students who need it the least—and *U.S. News* gives you high marks for that. I call it 'the greatest inefficiency ranking in America'" (Wermund 2017a).

Another popular explanation for college cost inflation involves a sophisticated pricing strategy called tuition discounting that an increasing number of institutions adopted beginning in the 1980s. Under this system, colleges and universities set artificially high prices for tuition and fees with the understanding that few students will end up paying the full published or "sticker" price. Tuition discounting allows admissions officers to negotiate with prospective students and offer them varying amounts of institutional aid, depending on their qualifications, to bring total costs down to an affordable level and entice them to enroll. Schools use tuition discounting to recruit high-achieving students, raise the quality of their student bodies, and bolster their reputations as elite academic institutions. Most colleges and universities offer their largest discounts in the form of merit-based scholarships. The academic criteria used in awarding these scholarships—such as grade point average, class rank, and standardized test scores—tend to correlate with family income. As a result, merit-based institutional aid often flows to students who could afford to attend college without it.

Need-based student financial aid, in contrast, has failed to keep pace with rising tuition rates. In 2019, the maximum federal Pell Grant amount of $6,095—provided to students with exceptional financial need—only covered 28 percent of the average published costs of tuition, fees, and room and board at public four-year universities, and 12 percent of the average published costs at private, nonprofit colleges (College Board 2020). Back in the 1970s, the maximum Pell Grant covered nearly 75 percent of the average cost of college (Goldrick-Rab et al. 2016). As schools have shifted their resources toward offering merit-based aid that primarily benefits middle- and upper-income students, undergraduates in the lowest income quartile face an average of $9,100 per year in unmet financial need (Pell Institute 2019).

Unequal Access and Outcomes

In addition to the expense associated with higher education, students from low-income families often face obstacles in the form of underperforming primary and secondary schools and inadequate resources to help them prepare for college admissions tests, fill out college applications, and apply for financial aid. In contrast, many students from wealthy families attend high-performing schools and enjoy access to advanced coursework, tutors, counselors, test-preparation services, and college admissions consultants. Affluent students also have more opportunities to enhance their college applications through participation in extracurricular activities and community service.

These factors contribute to significant income-based disparities in college enrollment. Among young people of similar academic ability, 80 percent of those from families in the top income quartile typically attend college, compared to only 30 percent from families in the bottom income quartile (Goldrick-Rab et al. 2016). Research also shows that wealthy students make up a disproportionate share of enrollment at highly selective U.S. colleges and universities, which draw more students from the top 1 percent family income bracket alone than from the entire bottom 60 percent (Taylor 2018). Enrollment at many taxpayer-funded, flagship public universities also lacks economic diversity. Although Pell Grant recipients comprise about 31 percent of all undergraduate students, for instance, they account for less than 20 percent of enrollment at the universities of Colorado, Michigan, Pennsylvania, and Virginia (Marcus 2017).

Studies also identify disparities in degree completion rates based on income levels. Many low-income students work long hours at part-time jobs to pay their living expenses, which can distract from their studies and increase the likelihood that they will leave college without earning a degree. In addition, surveys reveal that an estimated 40 percent of students on U.S. college campuses experience food insecurity—defined as limited or uncertain access to affordable, nutritious meals—as they struggle to afford the costs of higher education (Barboy 2019). As a result, only 15 percent of students with family incomes in the bottom quartile earn bachelor's degrees within ten years of graduating from high school, compared to 60 percent of students with family incomes in the top quartile (Zinshteyn 2016). Critics charge that the college affordability crisis thus perpetuates economic inequality and social stratification in the United States by making higher education—and the high-paying jobs that require degrees—the exclusive domain of young people from wealthy families. "We are creating a permanent underclass in America based on education—something we've never had before," said Brit Kirwan, former chancellor of the University of Maryland (Wermund 2017a).

Growing Student Loan Debt

The explosive growth in tuition costs, coupled with policies that encourage students and families to borrow money for college, triggered a steep rise in student loan debt. In fact, the amount of student debt outstanding has doubled since 2010 and quadrupled since 2004 (McHarris and Imani 2020). By 2019, total student loans reached a staggering $1.6 trillion, surpassing credit cards and auto loans and ranking behind only mortgage debt as the largest consumer financial obligation. The average cumulative loan balance for students who complete a bachelor's degree exceeds $30,000. "By almost any definition, this is a crisis," wrote Daniel M. Johnson in the *Harvard Business Review*. "It is certainly a crisis for those with student loan debts whose repayment schedules span decades, with large monthly payments. It is also a crisis for lenders experiencing significant default rates and, perhaps, a crisis for the federal government, as it guarantees these student loans. Many argue that it is also a crisis for our nation's economy; servicing this debt has a chilling effect on the sale of houses, cars, appliances, and furniture, as well as spending for vacations and luxury items" (Johnson 2019).

Some critics contend that U.S. government policies instigated the student debt crisis. In 1972, the federal government established the Student Loan Marketing Association (SLMA or Sallie Mae) to help students borrow money to pay for college. Lawmakers initially envisioned federally guaranteed student loans as a means of enabling young Americans to invest in their own financial futures. Loans provided access to college—and a pathway to better jobs and a more prosperous life—for students who might otherwise struggle to afford it. Yet critics charge that the introduction of federal student loans shifted the financial burden of higher education from the larger society onto individual students.

Over the next four decades, as both college costs and student loan debt skyrocketed, Sallie Mae and other major players in the student loan financing industry earned massive profits. According to consumer advocates, their success came at the expense of the nation's college graduates. Lenders and servicers of education loans used their financial resources to reshape the HEA and other education policies in their favor by eliminating basic protections for borrowers and bestowing themselves with unprecedented collection powers. For instance, industry lobbyists made student loans the only type of consumer debt that could not be discharged in bankruptcy, as well as the only type of loan obligation allowed to be garnished from borrowers' Social Security payments.

The lack of options for discharging education loans—along with accumulating interest, fees, penalties, and collection charges that can double or triple the original loan balance—contributes to high levels of default among student borrowers. As of 2018, around one million borrowers went into default on their federal student loans each year, and experts predicted that up 40 percent of all borrowers could enter default by 2023 (Nova 2018). Meanwhile, federal programs designed to provide borrowers with options for student debt relief, such as income-based repayment plans, merely extend the loan terms and force borrowers to continue making payments over longer periods of time. From 2010 through 2020, only about 3 percent of existing student loan balances were paid off each year. In fact, half of all borrowers who were scheduled to begin repaying federal student loans in 2010 had made no progress after five years (Kaur 2020). Slow repayment rates contributed to a 7 percent annual increase in the total outstanding debt balance, which economists predict may reach $3 trillion by 2030 (Johnson 2019).

Members of the millennial generation, who reached college age during the first two decades of the twenty-first century, rank among the individuals hardest hit by the student debt crisis. Many millennials graduated in the wake of the 2008 recession and found themselves facing poor employment prospects and mountains of student loan debt. Surveys show that millennials borrowed an average of 300 percent more than their parents (Hoffower 2019). Many borrowers find that the constant struggle to repay student loans affects their life choices for decades. College graduates with student debt tend to be less selective in the job market and accept part-time work for which they are overqualified. They also typically lack the financial security and risk tolerance to launch new business ventures. For many student borrowers, the need to pay down debt means postponing major life milestones, such as moving out of their parents' home, getting married, buying a house, starting a family, or saving for retirement. Student debt also exacts a toll on the U.S. economy by limiting the purchasing power of a generation of consumers.

Reforming Higher Education

The college affordability and student debt crises have raised questions about the value of higher education. In a 2019 Pew Research Center survey, half of adult respondents said that the U.S. higher education system had a generally positive impact on individuals and society. On the other hand, 38 percent disagreed—an increase of 12 points since 2012—and said higher education had a negative impact. In addition, nearly two-thirds of respondents felt that American higher education was heading in the wrong direction. Critics expressed concern about high tuition rates and student debt levels, questioned the fairness and equity of the college admissions process, raised doubts about whether college coursework prepared students for successful careers, and expressed reservations about university faculty members promoting liberal political views (Parker 2019).

For millennials, in particular, the college affordability and student debt crises have prompted a loss of confidence in higher education. Although 84 percent of millennials agreed that a college degree is necessary to get a good job and achieve a comfortable, middle-class lifestyle, only 13 percent said the American higher education system is effective in helping individuals reach their goals (Wermund 2017b). Many millennials believe that the system is rigged in favor of wealth and privilege and no longer provides ordinary people with an opportunity to achieve the American dream. "Higher education cannot be a luxury reserved just for a privileged few," said former president Barack Obama. "It is an economic necessity for every family. And every family should be able to afford it" (Obama 2012).

The college affordability and student debt crises also produced calls for higher education reform. In response, several 2020 Democratic presidential candidates proposed ambitious plans for tuition-free public college or student debt forgiveness. Other policymakers proposed free-market approaches that eliminate government funding for higher education. In the absence of fundamental changes to the system, the lack of college affordability and access appears likely to affect the choices of the next generation of students. A 2019 survey of college-age young people found that 20 percent thought about opting out of college, while 25 percent considered pursuing more affordable alternatives, such as taking online classes, starting out at a community college, or delaying college entry to work, save money, volunteer, or travel (TD Ameritrade 2019).

Affordable higher education, according to proponents, still holds the potential to benefit individuals and society by increasing workforce productivity, promoting technological development, raising tax revenues, fostering equality, reducing poverty, and helping citizens reach their potential and achieve the American dream. Some observers claim that students hold the key to determining the future of higher education. "We are long overdue for genuine, transformative reform. One source for leading a reform movement that we have not seriously considered is the students themselves. Students hold the power to force change in our colleges and universities," Daniel M. Johnson wrote. "Students ... have everything to gain by shaking up the status quo—their freedom, their financial futures, their mental health, and the power to help forge a new path that's no longer built on the backs of those that higher education seeks to serve" (Johnson 2019).

Further Reading

Alexander, F. King. 2016. "LSU President: If We Want Public Colleges to Be Affordable, a Federal-State Partnership Is Key."*Washington Post,* August 10, 2016. https://www.washingtonpost.com/news/grade-point/wp/2016/08/10/lsu-president-if-we-want-public-colleges-to-be-affordable-a-federal-state-partnership-is-key/.

Barboy, Dante. 2019. "What It Looks Like to Be Hungry in College." Center for American Progress, December 19, 2019. https://www.americanprogress.org/

issues/education-postsecondary/news/2019/12/19/478916/looks-like-hungry-college/.

Clinton, William J. 2000. "Remarks on Launching the Agenda for Higher Education and Lifelong Learning." January 20, 2000.*Public Papers of the Presidents of the United States: William J. Clinton, 2000-2001.* Washington, DC: Office of the Federal Register, National Archives and Records Administration.

College Board. 2020. "Pell Grants: Recipients, Maximum Pell, and Average Pell." https://research.collegeboard.org/trends/student-aid/figures-tables/pell-grants-recipients-maximum-pell-and-average-pell.

Connell, Kevin W. 2016. *Breaking Point: The College Affordability Crisis and Our Next Financial Bubble.* Lanham, MD: Rowman and Littlefield.

Goldrick-Rab, Sara, Robert Kelchen, Douglas N. Harris, and James Benson. 2016. "Reducing Income Inequality in Educational Attainment: Experimental Evidence on the Impact of Financial Aid on College Completion." *American Journal of Sociology* 121(6): 1762–1817. https://hope4college.com/wp-content/uploads/2018/09/Goldrick-Rab-etal-Reducing-Income-Inequality-in-Educational-Attainment.pdf.

Hoffower, Hillary. 2019. "2019 Is the Final Class of Millennial College Graduates. Next Stop: The Great American Affordability Crisis." *Business Insider,* May 22, 2019. https://www.businessinsider.com/millennials-last-graduating-class-affordability-crisis-student-loans-housing-2019-5.

Johnson, Daniel M. 2019. "What Will It Take to Solve the Student Loan Crisis?" *Harvard Business Review,* September 23, 2019. https://hbr.org/2019/09/what-will-it-take-to-solve-the-student-loan-crisis.

Johnson, Lyndon B. 1965. "Remarks on Signing the Higher Education Act of 1965." LBJ Presidential Library, November 8, 1965. http://www.lbjlibrary.org/mediakits/highereducation/p8.html.

Kaur, Harmeet. 2020. "The Student Loan Debt Is $1.6 Trillion and People Are Struggling to Pay It Down." CNN, January 19, 2020. https://www.cnn.com/2020/01/19/us/student-loan-slow-repayment-moodys-trnd/index.html.

Marcus, Jon. 2017. "In an Era of Inequity, More and More College Financial Aid Is Going to the Rich." Hechinger Report, December 7, 2017. https://hechingerreport.org/era-inequity-college-financial-aid-going-rich/.

McHarris, Philip V., and Zellie Imani. 2020. "It Is Time to Cancel Student Debt and Make Higher Education Free." *Al Jazeera,* April 26, 2020.

National Center for Education Statistics. 2020. "Undergraduate Enrollment." Institute of Education Sciences, May 2020. https://nces.ed.gov/programs/coe/indicator_cha.asp.

Nova, Annie. 2018. "More Than One Million People Default on Their Student Loans Each Year." CNBC, August 13, 2018. https://www.cnbc.com/2018/08/13/twenty-two-percent-of-student-loan-borrowers-fall-into-default.html.

Obama, Barack. 2012. "Remarks by the President on College Affordability." The White House, June 21, 2012. https://obamawhitehouse.archives.gov/the-press-office/2012/06/21/remarks-president-college-affordability.

Parker, Kim. 2019. "The Growing Partisan Divide in Views of Higher Education." Pew Research Center, August 19, 2019. https://www.pewsocialtrends.org/essay/the-growing-partisan-divide-in-views-of-higher-education/.

Pell Institute. 2019. "Indicators of Higher Education Equity in the United States: 2019 Historical Trend Report." http://pellinstitute.org/downloads/publications-Indicators_of_Higher_Education_Equity_in_the_US_2019_Historical_Trend_Report.pdf.

Powell, Farran, and Emma Kerr. 2019. "See the Average College Tuition in 2019-2020." *U.S. News*, September 9, 2019. https://www.usnews.com/education/best-colleges/paying-for-college/articles/paying-for-college-infographic.

Selingo, Jeffrey J. 2016. "The Biggest Problem Facing Higher Education, in One Chart." *Washington Post*, March 8, 2016. https://www.washingtonpost.com/news/grade-point/wp/2016/03/08/the-biggest-problem-facing-higher-education-in-one-chart/?noredirect=on.

Taylor, Kelley. 2018. "College Affordability Guides Provoke Debate, Action on Economic Inequality on Campus." *Insight into Diversity,* October 18, 2018. https://www.insightintodiversity.com/college-affordability-guides-provoke-debate-action-on-economic-inequality-on-campuses/.

TD Ameritrade. 2019. "Young Americans and College Survey." August 2019. https://s2.q4cdn.com/437609071/files/doc_news/research/2019/young-americans-and-college-survey.pdf.

U.S. Congress Joint Economic Committee. 2017. "The College Affordability Crisis in America." https://www.jec.senate.gov/public/_cache/files/5270bffa-c68e-44f0-ac08-693485083747/the-college-affordability-crisis-in-america.pdf.

Watson, Patrick W. 2019. "OK Boomers, About That Working-through-College Thing." *Forbes,* December 9, 2019. https://www.forbes.com/sites/patrickw-watson/2019/12/09/ok-boomers-about-that-working-through-college-thing/#79489b2f2e86.

Wermund, Benjamin. 2017a. "How U.S. News College Rankings Promote Economic Inequality on Campus." Politico, September 10, 2017. https://www.politico.com/interactives/2017/top-college-rankings-list-2017-us-news-investigation/.

Wermund, Benjamin. 2017b. "Losing Faith in Higher Education." Politico, May 11, 2017. https://www.politico.com/tipsheets/morning-education/2017/05/losing-faith-in-higher-education-220254.

Zinshteyn, Mikhail. 2016. "The Growing College-Degree Wealth Gap." *Atlantic,* April 25, 2016. https://www.theatlantic.com/education/archive/2016/04/the-growing-wealth-gap-in-who-earns-college-degrees/479688/.

CHAPTER TWO

Landmark Events

This chapter explores important milestones and events in the ongoing debate over college affordability and student loan debt in the United States. It traces the history of higher education, examines the reasons why college costs rose much faster than inflation beginning in the 1980s, and charts the concurrent growth in student borrowing and debt loads. It also explores the increasing popularity of for-profit colleges in the early twenty-first century, as well as the federal government's efforts to regulate the industry. Finally, it analyzes the ways in which the college admissions system favors wealthy applicants, contributes to social stratification, and drives public demands for higher education reform.

History of Higher Education in the United States (1636-1980s)

Higher education in the United States—as delivered through around 4,000 degree-granting postsecondary institutions across the country—ranked as the best in the world in 2018, according to the QS Higher Education System Strength Rankings (B2B Marketing 2019). American institutions of higher learning also claimed 7 of the top 10 spots in the *Times Higher Education* World University Rankings for 2020. Historians noted that the academic excellence of major American colleges and universities produced scholarship that contributed to the economic prosperity, military strength, and cultural influence of the United States.

Unlike the higher education systems in most other countries, U.S. postsecondary education evolved without a formal plan or central coordination. Instead, it evolved naturally over time to form a decentralized network of diverse institutions—ranging from giant public research universities to tiny private liberal arts colleges—that served around

17 million undergraduate students and 3 million graduate students in the 2019-2020 academic year (Institute of Education Sciences 2019).

Early Institutions of Higher Learning

Puritan leaders of the Massachusetts Bay Colony founded the first institution of higher learning in the American colonies, Harvard University, in 1636 to train members of the clergy and promote their religious beliefs. They modeled the school upon the venerable Oxford and Cambridge universities in England, which had already existed for more than five centuries by that time. Several other American colonies chartered colleges during the 1700s, bringing the total to nine prior to independence. Seven of these institutions eventually became members of the Ivy League. The colonial colleges—especially Princeton University in New Jersey—served as hotbeds of political dissent and revolutionary sentiment that led to the rebellion against British rule. Colonial college alumni served as military commanders during the American Revolution and as statesmen in crafting a system of government for the United States. By 1790, when Rhode Island became the last of the original 13 states to ratify the U.S. Constitution, the new nation boasted 19 institutions of higher learning. This list included Transylvania University in Kentucky, which became the first college on the western frontier upon its founding in 1780 and went on to produce a large number of influential political figures.

Once the federal government took shape, some founders pushed to create a national university for the United States. George Washington and other prominent leaders argued that such an institution, modeled after the prestigious universities of Europe, would generate knowledge and help unify the country. Opponents, on the other hand, criticized the scheme as undemocratic, claiming that it infringed on states' rights to create their own systems and preserved higher education as a privilege for the wealthy elite. After the national university idea fell by the wayside, another key development occurred in 1819, when the U.S. Supreme Court weighed in to settle a dispute concerning the governance of Dartmouth College. The justices ruled that the state of New Hampshire, which had granted Dartmouth a charter as a public corporation, could not interfere in the school's operation. The guarantee of freedom from state control led to a college-building boom, with more than 200 new institutions of higher learning arising between 1800 and 1850.

Wealthy philanthropists founded a number of renowned schools during the 1800s, such as Duke, Johns Hopkins, Vanderbilt, and Stanford universities. As the nation expanded westward, many cities and states established liberal arts colleges to serve as community centers, attract residents, and increase land values. Mount Holyoke in Massachusetts became the first women's college upon its founding in 1837. That same year, Oberlin College in Ohio became the first co-educational institution as well as the first to admit African American students. As the number of colleges and universities grew, the curricula offered also began to shift away from liberal arts and classical languages to include more technical areas of study, such as engineering, science, and medicine.

The federal government increased its involvement in higher education in 1862, when Congress passed the Morrill Land Grant Colleges Act. The legislation's main proponent, Representative Justin Smith Morrill of Vermont, was the self-taught son of a blacksmith who regretted his lack of formal education and wanted to expand access to college and professional careers. Signed by President Abraham Lincoln in the absence of southern legislators during the Civil War, the act allotted tracts of federal land in the West to states based on their populations. The states agreed to use the profits as an endowment to support "at least one college where the leading object shall be ... to teach such branches of learning as are related to agriculture and the mechanic arts ... in order to promote the liberal and practical education of the industrial classes on the several pursuits and professions in life" (Geiger 2015, 281).

In effect, the Morrill Act provided federal funding for higher education in practical, applied fields of study, including agriculture, science, engineering, and military arts. Although some states used the funds to add such programs at established colleges, most created new institutions that became known as land-grant colleges or state universities. By 1880, the number of institutions of higher learning in the United States exceeded 800—more than five times as many as in all of Europe (Labaree 2017). In 1890, Congress passed a second Morrill Act that earmarked federal funds to increase educational opportunities for African Americans. Although this funding supported the creation of Historically Black Colleges and Universities (HBCU) in the South, critics charged that it also signaled federal acceptance of racial segregation in education. With their emphasis on science and technology, the land-grant colleges contributed to a trend toward industrialization and urbanization at the turn of the twentieth century. In 1900, the presidents of 14 prominent research institutions formed the Association of American Universities to demonstrate their commitment to promoting discoveries that advanced society.

Higher Education's Golden Age

Enrollment in higher education declined during World War I (1914-1918) and World War II (1939-1945) as millions of college-aged men and women served in the U.S. armed forces. American universities contributed to the war efforts, however, through scientific and technological research that led to military advancements. In 1944, Congress passed the Servicemen's Readjustment Act to provide financial benefits to help returning military personnel build successful civilian lives. Better known as the G.I. Bill, it included an education benefit that provided veterans with tuition and living expenses toward higher education or vocational training. More than 2 million veterans took advantage of the program to attend colleges or universities by the time it expired in 1956. Historians credited the G.I. Bill for increasing public acceptance of postsecondary education as a path to join the growing American middle class.

Federal government officials also recognized the value of higher education to the nation's economy and interests during the postwar era. During the Cold War, as the United States expanded its national defense spending to compete with the Soviet Union, institutions of higher learning received funding for programs in chemistry, physics, engineering, political science, and foreign languages. The federal government also pursued policies aimed at expanding college access and affordability as a means of increasing national competitiveness. Some of these efforts grew out of recommendations made by the Commission on Higher Education, convened in 1946 by President Harry S. Truman to examine "the functions of higher education in our democracy and the means by which they can best be performed" (Thelin 2011, 268).

To meet the commission's goal of "expanding educational opportunities for all able young people," the higher education system developed a network of public community colleges to accommodate increased enrollment by the postwar baby-boom generation. These institutions offered two-year associate's degrees in certain occupational fields and also enabled students to transfer to four-year colleges and universities after completing preliminary coursework. The network eventually expanded to include more than 1,500 community colleges nationwide and helped total postsecondary enrollment grow from 1.5 million in 1940 to 7.9 million in 1970 (Thelin 2011, 261).

During the turbulent 1960s and 1970s, college campuses became the center of student-led social activism in the civil rights movement, the women's liberation movement, the free speech movement, and the antiwar movement. In 1960, for instance, four black students from North Carolina A&T University sat down at a whites-only Woolworth's lunch counter in Greensboro, launching a nationwide series of sit-in protests against segregated public facilities. College-age members of the Student Nonviolent Coordinating Committee played a prominent role in many other civil rights demonstrations, including the Freedom Rides to desegregate interstate bus systems and Freedom Summer to register black voters in the South. Opposition to U.S. involvement in the Vietnam War also converged on college campuses, where military draft-age activists with Students for a Democratic Society and other groups occupied buildings, organized protest marches, and burned draft cards. College-age women also participated in demonstrations to support passage of the Equal Rights Amendment and Title IX of the Education Amendments of 1972, which prohibited sex discrimination at educational institutions that received federal funding.

As college degrees became requirements for an increasing number of occupations, the federal government introduced student financial aid programs to help low-income students afford the rising costs of tuition. The Higher Education Act (HEA) of 1965, for instance, established the Guaranteed Student Loan program (precursor to the Stafford Loan program), which partnered with banks to provide low-interest loans to enable students with demonstrated financial need to attend college. In his remarks on signing the legislation, President Lyndon Johnson declared that, "for the individual, education is the path to achievement and fulfillment; for the Nation, it is a path to a society that is not only free but civilized; and for the world, it is the path to peace—for it is education that places reason over force" (Johnson 1965). Later amendments and reauthorizations of the HEA loosened federal loan eligibility requirements to include middle-income students, increased borrowing limits, and allowed lenders to charge fees.

In 1979, President Jimmy Carter signed legislation creating the Department of Education (DOE) as a separate, Cabinet-level department. Although state governments took the lead in establishing and overseeing colleges and universities, the DOE provided funding to postsecondary students in the form of grants, loans, and work-study opportunities. By 2019, the DOE budget included $130 billion in financial aid to help 11.5 million students afford college (U.S. Secretary of Education 2018). Federal spending on higher education emerged as a controversial topic soon after the creation of the DOE. William J. Bennett, who became secretary of education in 1985, endorsed President Ronald Reagan's proposal for dramatic cuts in financial aid expenditures. Bennett famously claimed that all but the neediest college students could afford tuition by making "a stereo divestiture, an automobile divestiture, or a three-weeks-at-the-beach divestiture" (Bates 1988). Some critics claimed that the availability of federal aid funding encouraged institutions of higher learning to increase tuition rates. Rising tuition rates, meanwhile, led to new questions about the mission of higher education and whether the cost was justified in terms of students' job skills, employability, and earning power.

Further Reading

Bates, Andrew J. 1988. "Bye Bye Wild Bill." *Harvard Crimson,* September 21, 1988. https://www.thecrimson.com/article/1988/9/21/bye-bye-wild-bill-pbabfter-three-and-a-half/.

B2B Marketing. 2019. "The Strongest Higher Education Systems by Country." QS.com, 2019. https://www.qs.com/the-strongest-higher-education-systems-by-country-overview/.

Geiger, Roger L. 2015. *The History of American Higher Education.* Princeton, NJ: Princeton University Press.

Institute of Education Sciences. 2019. "Fast Facts." National Center for Education Statistics, 2019. https://nces.ed.gov/fastfacts/display.asp?id=372#College_enrollment.

Johnson, Lyndon B. 1965. "Remarks on Signing the Higher Education Act," November 8, 1965. http://www.lbjlibrary.org/mediakits/highereducation/.

Labaree, David F. 2017. *A Perfect Mess: The Unlikely Ascendancy of Higher Education.* Chicago and London: University of Chicago Press.

Mintz, Steven. 2017. "Eleven Lessons from the History of Higher Ed." *Inside Higher Ed,* May 7, 2017. https://www.insidehighered.com/blogs/higher-ed-gamma/11-lessons-history-higher-ed.

Thelin, John R. 2011. *A History of American Higher Education.* 2d ed. Baltimore, MD: Johns Hopkins University Press.

U.S. Secretary of Education. 2018. "Education Department FY2019 Budget." U.S. Department of Education, February 14, 2018. https://www2.ed.gov/about/overview/budget/budget19/budget-factsheet.pdf.

"World University Rankings 2020." *Times Higher Education,* 2020. https://www.timeshighereducation.com/world-university-rankings/2020/world-ranking#survey-answer.

A Sociologist Questions the Value of Higher Education (1979)

The importance of higher education in American society rose steadily following World War II, as millions of people came to view a college degree as a vital prerequisite to getting a good job and achieving upward mobility. From the 1950s through the 1970s, institutions of higher learning increased in number, size, and diversity of academic programs to accommodate the demands of rapidly growing student populations. Most observers viewed these changes as positive, arguing that education gave individuals the ability to raise their social status and also advanced national interests by driving technological innovation and economic growth. "Every American benefits when every other American has access to as much schooling as he or she wants," Adam Davidson wrote in *New York Times Magazine.*

"In an economy that demands and rewards education, those who have it will pay the bills for those who don't" (Davidson 2015).

In 1979, sociologist Randall Collins became one of the first experts to challenge conventional notions about the value of higher education. His book *The Credential Society: A Historical Sociology of Education and Stratification* examined trends in higher education with a critical eye and questioned whether the American system truly benefitted individuals and society. Collins traced a cycle of "credential inflation," in which employers required higher and higher levels of education for workers to perform the same jobs. He claimed that this phenomenon caused advanced degrees to diminish in value over time, which in turn meant that higher education did not promote social mobility. Although Collins's arguments were "considered scandalous" at the time of publication (Collins 2018), his book eventually came to be considered a classic in its field for accurately predicting some of the problems that faced higher education four decades later. In recognition of its continuing relevance, Columbia University Press reissued *The Credential Society* in a "Legacy Edition" with new forewords in 2019.

Credential Inflation and Social Mobility

Collins's work upended some of the ideas put forth by sociologists in the 1950s and 1960s about the relationship between education and social class. "Research on social mobility (now called status attainment) found that the strongest predictor of a child's future job was the education of his or her parents," Collins explained. "So the theory of meritocracy was developed: if a child could get more education than one's parents, he/she would end up in a higher social class" (Collins 2018). Under this theory, expanding access to higher education would create a more fair and equal society. Proponents supported policies and programs aimed at enabling women, minorities, and students from low-income families to attend college.

Collins challenged the widely accepted view of higher education as a public good that could reduce social stratification. Instead, he argued that the value of advanced degrees diminished as more people attained them because businesses demanded ever-higher educational qualifications for the same positions. "In the U.S., the value of a 12-year (high school) diploma now is almost worthless for getting a job; it is only useful for entry into university to get a higher degree," Collins noted. "Jobs that formerly had lower requirements, like police officer, now require a college degree, while a [master's degree] in criminology or criminal justice is required to become a police chief.... This has happened all across the spectrum of jobs" (Collins 2018).

Collins called this phenomenon "credential inflation" and claimed that it prevented gains in educational access and attainment from leading to social equality. "Educational credential inflation expands on false premises—the ideology that more education will produce more equality of opportunity, more high-tech economic performance, and more good jobs," he wrote in the preface to the Legacy Edition. "Social class mobility in the United States has been stagnant since the mid-twentieth century, unaffected by the huge increase in levels of education over that period" (Collins 2019, xi). Supporters of Collins's theory criticized policies and programs intended to provide broader access to higher education, calling them misguided and unlikely to result in socioeconomic gains. "We are deceiving our young population to mindlessly pursue college degrees when very often that is advice that is increasingly questionable," noted a writer for the *Chronicle of Higher Education* (Vedder 2010).

Collins predicted that the cycle of credential inflation would produce an affordability crisis in higher education. He argued that social pressures to expand college access fostered competition between institutions and led to uncontrolled growth in the higher-education industry. To attract more students, institutions expanded their academic offerings to include narrow, specialized areas of study. They passed the cost of these highly focused courses on to students and their parents in the form of tuition increases. As the value of higher education declined, students spent more years in college pursuing advanced degrees, incurred more costs and student-loan debt, and delayed their entry into the productive workforce. Eventually, this cycle raised questions about whether the investment required to earn credentials was worthwhile. "The cost of college and professional schools has grown far faster than the rate of inflation in the economy," Collins wrote. "Education administrators could get away with increasingly higher prices because of credential inflation, which increases the number of applicants competing for a chance at the most prestigious degrees. Student loans put off the reckoning, but at some point it becomes economically infeasible to sustain the inflationary spiral inside the credential-producing sector" (Collins 2019, xii).

Higher Education and Tech Jobs

The Credential Society also examined the reasons behind credential inflation. Collins disputed the prevailing theory among sociologists, which attributed the continual growth in employment qualifications to advances in technology that required workers to possess ever-greater technical skills. "The technological theory of education … said that modern jobs become more complex and more technical, so in order to get a job in the modern sector one needs more education," he explained. "I found that the high-tech organizations of the time (i.e., the 1960s) had lower educational requirements than low-tech organizations; and that higher credential requirements were in high status organizations (such as elite law firms)" (Collins 2018).

Collins asserted that higher education did not provide the technical skills workers needed in high-tech jobs. Instead, he claimed that workers tended to acquire these skills through informal experience and on-the-job training. Under his theory, students pursued advanced degrees not to gain technical skills, but as a means of signaling to employers that they had the capacity to acquire those skills once hired. Employers, meanwhile, used educational credentials as a means of screening potential employees and limiting the number of applicants for positions. Collins further posited that formal education did not necessarily increase workers' productivity. "Job skill cannot be assumed to be related to educational levels in a simple linear fashion," he wrote. "Beyond certain [educational] plateaus the relationships may well be reversed," because "better educated employees are more likely to be dissatisfied with jobs and to change jobs more often than less educated persons" (Craig 2019).

Some critics called Collins's arguments out of date, arguing that they no longer applied in the fast-paced, global, technology-driven business environment of the twenty-first century. "This is a work that was only possible before the digital revolution," Ryan Craig wrote in *Inside Higher Ed.* "Educated workers are not only more productive in a digital environment, but without the requisite degrees (and increasingly skills), they won't be hired and may well be invisible to hiring managers by dint of applicant-tracking system software" (Craig 2019). Craig pointed to the results of a survey indicating that 61 percent of all full-time, entry-level employment opportunities required at least three years of experience. He argued that employers no longer offered on-the-job training and instead expected candidates to possess the necessary qualifications to perform immediately. "A more relevant and pressing question for academics like Collins," according to Craig, "is whether the educational approaches currently prized by America's colleges and universities are sufficient for developing the necessary cognitive skills for interacting productively with future digital technologies, or whether new pedagogies, curricula, programs, and pathways will be required. Whoever gets this right will be have a massive market for their credentials" (Craig 2019).

Collins cited the examples of such information technology pioneers as Steve Jobs—who dropped out of college to invent Apple computers—as evidence that educational credentials remained irrelevant in the digital age. "This has been the pattern with the entrepreneurs who created Facebook, Google, Tesla, and others by exploiting the technological edge," he wrote. "School systems standardize what has already happened; that is the reason dropouts who seize the opportunities for innovation directly have greater success than those who follow the bureaucratic path through the step-by-step of required years in school" (Collins 2019, x).

Further Reading

Collins, Randall. 2018. "Educational Credential Inflation: An Interview with Randall Collins." The Sociological Eye (blog), July 19, 2018. http://sociological-eye.blogspot.com/2018/07/educational-credential-inflation.html.

Collins, Randall. 2019. *The Credential Society: A Historical Sociology of Education and Stratification.* Legacy Edition. New York: Columbia University Press.

Craig, Ryan. 2019. "Technology 1, 'Credential Society' 0." *Inside Higher Ed,* July 24, 2019. https://www.insidehighered.com/digital-learning/views/2019/07/24/1979-book-arguing-education-about-credentialing-not-skills-rings.

Davidson, Adam. 2015. "Is College Tuition Really Too High?" *New York Times Magazine,* September 13, 2015. https://www.nytimes.com/2015/09/13/magazine/is-college-tuition-too-high.html?_r=1.

Labaree, David F. 1997. *How to Succeed in School without Really Learning: The Credentials Race in American Education.* New Haven, CT: Yale University Press.

Vedder, Richard. 2010. "The Great College-Degree Scam." *Chronicle of Higher Education,* December 9, 2010. https://www.chronicle.com/blogs/innovations/the-great-college-degree-scam/28067.

Escalation in College Costs (1980s-2000s)

For decades, U.S. leaders promoted higher education as a worthwhile investment that enabled Americans to increase their future earnings potential and contribute to the nation's economic growth. The promise of higher-paying jobs and greater social mobility encouraged millions of people to go to college. As of 2016, U.S. Census figures showed that 33 percent of Americans over age 25 had earned at least a bachelor's degree, compared to less than 5 percent in 1940 (Wilson 2017). In addition, adults who completed a four-year college degree earned an average of $30,000 more per year than adults with only a high school diploma, which translated to around $1 million more over the course of a lifetime (Davidson 2015).

Despite the potential benefits, however, a college degree remained out of reach for many Americans. Beginning in the 1980s, the cost of higher education grew three to four times faster than the overall rate of inflation in the

U.S. economy. As a result, the average published cost to earn a four-year degree at colleges and universities nationwide more than doubled within three decades—even when adjusted for inflation—to reach $104,500 in 2016 (Maldanado 2018). Since median annual wages remained stagnant during this period, a year of college that accounted for 22 percent of an average family's annual income in 1989 required 45 percent of that family's yearly income in 2016 (Selingo 2016). Skyrocketing tuition costs raised questions about the value of higher education and placed pressure on lawmakers and administrators to find ways to make college more affordable.

Education Becomes Less Affordable

The rapid escalation in tuition costs started in the 1980s, around the time the tail end of the postwar baby-boom generation reached college age. When adjusted for inflation, annual tuition for in-state students at public, four-year universities averaged $3,200 in 1987. By 2017, these same universities charged students nearly $10,000 in annual tuition—an increase of 213 percent in 30 years. Similarly, annual tuition at private, nonprofit colleges averaged $15,200 in inflation-adjusted dollars in 1987. The published tuition rates for these schools grew to nearly $35,000 annually by 2017—a 129 percent increase (Martin 2017).

The parents of today's college students often scraped together enough money to cover a year's tuition by working at summer jobs. With the explosive growth in tuition costs, however, members of the millennial generation were forced to rely on financial aid in the form of scholarships, grants, on-campus employment, and student loans. The National Center for Education Statistics reported that 46 percent of newly enrolled, full-time undergraduate students took out loans in academic year 2016-2017, with an average loan amount of $7,200. Among students who completed a bachelor's degree that year, the average cumulative loan balance reached $31,200 (National Center for Education Statistics 2019). Many young people struggled for years to pay off their student loan debts, which often forced them to delay or forego such financial goals as buying homes and saving for retirement.

The rising costs of higher education had a disproportionate impact on young people from low-income families, for whom attending college became prohibitively expensive. Critics charged that the college affordability crisis perpetuated social stratification in the United States by making higher education—and high-paying jobs—the exclusive domain of young people from wealthy families. "Without greater access to higher education, the United States is likely to have even greater income inequality," Adam Davidson wrote in *New York Times Magazine*. "A huge segment of the population will see its income fall and some of our core assumptions about national identity—ours as a land of opportunity, a prosperous democracy —will be at risk" (Davidson 2015).

Rising college costs, coupled with stagnant wages, contributed to a decline in public confidence about the value of higher education. In a 2017 survey, for instance, 40 percent of respondents agreed that "pursuing a college degree is not a worthwhile investment" for most high school students because of poor job prospects and high student loan debt (Lederman 2017). Such questions, in turn, threatened efforts by U.S. leaders to build an educated populace to promote economic growth. Prior to 1980, studies showed that the average level of educational attainment increased by two years for each generation of Americans, which helped the United States rank as the most-educated country in the world. Over the next few decades, however, U.S. education levels lagged behind other industrialized nations, and by 2015 educational attainment among Americans between the ages of 25 and 34 ranked fourteenth in the world (Davidson 2015).

Explanations for Rising College Costs

Analysts pointed to a variety of factors to explain the rapid increase in college costs since the 1980s. Public universities, in particular, often cited declining state funding for higher education as a major contributor to rising tuition rates. Many states struggled to balance their budgets in the 1990s and early 2000s in the face of increasing expenses for health care, social services, infrastructure, and other items. These problems grew more severe during the economic recession that began in 2007, when most states saw their tax revenues drop precipitously. Many state governments responded by cutting funding for higher education, which declined by an average of 25 percent per student nationwide from 2000 to 2015 (Davidson 2015). University administrators argued that the lower state funding forced them to raise tuition and fees, thus shifting the burden onto students and their parents. The portion of public-college revenue generated from student tuition grew from 37 percent in 2008 to 46 percent in 2017 (Mulhere 2018).

Some analysts rejected this explanation for rising tuition rates, however, pointing out that state legislative appropriations for higher education increased over time—although not as much as tuition rates. When adjusted for inflation, state funding for colleges and universities grew from $48.2 billion in 1975 to $86.6 billion in 2009. While funding dipped during the recession, it recovered to reach $94.5 billion by 2017 (Mulhere 2018). Critics blamed the apparent drop in per-student state funding on the fact that more young people chose to pursue higher education, especially when the recession limited their job opportunities. "Enrollment in undergraduate, graduate and professional programs has increased by almost 50 percent since 1995," Paul F. Campos wrote in the *New York Times*. "As a consequence, while state legislative appropriations for higher education have risen much faster than inflation, total state appropriations per student are somewhat lower than they were at their peak in 1990.... It is disingenuous to call a large increase in public spending a 'cut,' as some university administrators do, because a huge programmatic expansion features somewhat lower per capita subsidies" (Campos 2015).

Some analysts blamed rising tuition and fees on a nationwide campus construction boom, as many prominent institutions of higher learning sought to appeal to prospective students and faculty members by offering the finest facilities and amenities. "Some colleges have doubled down in a competition for students that involves fancy dorms, high-end student centers, climbing walls, and lazy rivers—paying for those amenities with still higher tuition and fees," said Senator Elizabeth Warren (D-MA) (Pallardy 2019). In 2017, colleges and universities nationwide spent a record $11.5 billion on construction projects (Green 2019). Louisiana State University spent $85 million to install a lazy river in the shape of the school's initials in its student recreation complex (Pallardy 2019).

Critics noted that many of these construction projects—such as gourmet dining facilities, state-of-the-art recreation and fitness centers, and luxurious dormitories—had nothing to do with the quality of education provided at various institutions. Instead, they claimed that the fancy new amenities amounted to vanity projects that mainly served to increase a school's prestige and differentiate it from its competitors. College administrators, on the other hand, portrayed campus construction projects as necessary expenditures to maintain, modernize, retrofit, or replace aging buildings and infrastructure. They noted that construction costs accounted for a small percentage of overall college budgets, and they also pointed to studies indicating that improvements in campus facilities made economic sense by helping to increase student enrollment and retention (Pallardy 2019).

Some analysts attributed the astronomical increases in college tuition rates to a trend among institutions to expand the size of their administrative staffs. The U.S. Department of Education reported that the number of full-time administrative positions at the nation's colleges and universities grew by 60 percent between 1993 and 2009. In the California state university system alone, the total number of administrators increased from 3,800 in 1975 to 12,183 in 2008 (Campos 2015). Critics noted that, unlike faculty members, administrators had little direct impact on the quality of education offered by universities. Instead, colleges hired additional administrative staff to handle fundraising, recruiting, academic counseling, financial aid, facility maintenance, and other services. Yet some analysts downplayed administrative bloat as a contributing factor to tuition increases, arguing that larger administrative staffs were needed to accommodate increases in student enrollment.

Other experts mentioned higher administrative salaries as a factor driving tuition inflation. The *Chronicle of Higher Education* reported that the average annual salary for a U.S. college president exceeded $500,000 in 2018. Some institutions paid their top administrators significantly more. The highest-paid public university president made $4.3 million in 2018, while the highest-paid private college president received $4.9 million (Pallardy 2019). Although salaries for full-time, tenured professors at the nation's top universities rose 12 percent faster than inflation from 2000 to 2018, average faculty salaries remained stagnant during this period because the number of full-time college professors declined (Green 2019). Many universities shifted toward employing lower-paid, part-time, adjunct faculty members. As a result, part-time faculty accounted for more than half of all college professors in 2015, compared to only 22 percent in 1970 (Davidson 2015).

Another possible explanation for rising tuition rates originated with William J. Bennett, who served as secretary of education from 1985 to 1988 under President Ronald Reagan. In a 1987 opinion piece for the *New York Times* entitled "Our Greedy Colleges," Bennett famously challenged the assertion that universities had to increase tuition to make up for decreases in federal financial aid to students. He pointed out that federal student aid payments had increased by 57 percent since 1980—or more than twice the rate of inflation over that period—yet tuition rates had increased as well. "Higher education is not underfunded," Bennett declared. "It is under-accountable and under-productive. Our students deserve better than this. They deserve an education commensurate with the large sums paid by parents and taxpayers and donors" (Bennett 1987).

Building upon this argument—known as the Bennett hypothesis—other analysts drew parallels between the expansion of federal student loan programs in the 1980s and the skyrocketing costs of college tuition since that time. They argued that the increased availability of federal student aid eliminated incentives for colleges and universities to keep their costs low. Instead, they claimed that it encouraged institutions to raise tuition rates by enabling students to borrow enough money to cover the higher costs. "College students and their families are at the mercy of the federal government and colleges everywhere," Douglas Green wrote in *Education Week Teacher*. "Student aid may cover more of the tuition, but if the aid wasn't available, tuition might not have gone up in the first place" (Green 2019). Other analysts expressed doubt about a causal relationship between federal aid and tuition increases, however, pointing out that tuition rose dramatically even during periods when federal loans did not (Pallardy 2019).

Another popular explanation for tuition inflation involved a sophisticated pricing strategy adopted by many colleges and universities beginning in the 1980s. An increasing number of schools used a system known as tuition discounting to recruit high-achieving students, raise the quality of their student bodies, and bolster their reputations as elite academic institutions. "Students are not just customers; they are also an integral part of the core product," Davidson explained. "When considering a school, potential students and their parents often look first at the characteristics of past classes: test scores, grade-point averages, post-college earnings, as well as ethnic and gender mixes. School admissions officers call the process through which they put together their classes the 'shaping' of the student body" (Davidson 2015).

Tuition discounting facilitated the process of shaping enrollment by giving admissions officers room to negotiate with prospective students. Under this system, colleges and universities set artificially high prices for tuition and fees—with the understanding that few students would end up paying the full published or "sticker" price. Then they offered varying amounts of institutional aid, depending on the qualifications of the student in question, to reduce the tuition rate to an affordable level and entice that student to enroll. The higher the published tuition price, the larger the discounts a school could offer desirable students. "To the public, one number is released: the cost of tuition. But internally the school likely has dozens of price points, each set for a different group of potential students," Davidson wrote. "A school that charges $50,000 is able to offer a huge range of inducements to different sorts of students. Some could pay $10,000, others $30,000 or $40,000" (Davidson 2015).

Since only wealthy, out-of-state, and international students typically paid the full price to attend, some critics referred to tuition discounting as a "soak the rich" scheme. Yet they also noted that most colleges and universities offered their largest discounts in the form of merit-based scholarships to highly qualified students. The academic criteria used in awarding these scholarships—such as grade point average, class rank, and standardized test scores—tended to correlate with family income. As a result, merit-based institutional aid often flowed to students who could afford to attend college without it. "High-achieving students from educated families receive a disproportionate share of financial assistance, while those at the bottom, struggling students from families ill equipped to support their educations, receive a disproportionately small share," Davidson stated. "There is enough money already out there to support everybody's education. The problem is that aid is distributed unevenly" (Davidson 2015).

Further Reading

Bennett, William J. 1987. "Our Greedy Colleges." *New York Times,* February 18, 1987. https://www.nytimes.com/1987/02/18/opinion/our-greedy-colleges.html.

Campos, Paul F. 2015. "The Real Reason College Tuition Costs So Much." *New York Times,* April 4, 2015. https://www.nytimes.com/2015/04/05/opinion/sunday/the-real-reason-college-tuition-costs-so-much.html.

Davidson, Adam. 2015. "Is College Tuition Really Too High?" *New York Times Magazine,* September 13, 2015. https://www.nytimes.com/2015/09/13/magazine/is-college-tuition-too-high.html?_r=1

Green, Douglas. 2019. "Why Has the Cost of College Outpaced Inflation?" *Education Week Teacher,* April 18, 2019. http://blogs.edweek.org/teachers/work_-in_progress/2019/04/why_has_the_cost_of_college_ou.html.

Lederman, Doug. 2017. "Is Higher Education Really Losing the Public?" *Inside Higher Ed,* December 15, 2017. https://www.insidehighered.com/news/2017/12/15/public-really-losing-faith-higher-education.

Maldonado, Camilo. 2018. "Price of College Increasing Almost 8 Times Faster Than Wages." *Forbes,* July 24, 2018. https://www.forbes.com/sites/camilo-maldonado/2018/07/24/price-of-college-increasing-almost-8-times-faster-than-wages/#7ea381c66c1d.

Martin, Emmie. 2017. "Here's How Much More Expensive It Is for You to Go to College Than It Was for Your Parents." CNBC, November 29, 2017. https://www.cnbc.com/2017/11/29/how-much-college-tuition-has-increased-from-1988-to-2018.html.

Mulhere, Kaitlin. 2018. "A Growing Number of States Are Spending Less on Public College Students." *Money,* March 29, 2018. https://money.com/state-public-college-funding-cuts-2017/.

National Center for Education Statistics. 2019. "Loans for Undergraduate Students." Institute for Education Sciences, May 2019. https://nces.ed.gov/programs/coe/indicator_cub.asp.

Pallardy, Richard. 2019. "Are Lavish Facilities Responsible for Tuition Inflation?" SavingForCollege.com, May 16, 2019. https://www.savingforcollege.com/article/are-lavish-facilities-responsible-for-tuition-inflation.

Selingo, Jeffrey J. 2016. "The Biggest Problem Facing Higher Education, in One Chart." *Washington Post,* March 8, 2016. https://www.washingtonpost.com/news/grade-point/wp/2016/03/08/the-biggest-problem-facing-higher-education-in-one-chart/?noredirect=on.

Wilson, Reid. 2017. "Census: More Americans Have College Degrees Than Ever Before." *The Hill,* April 3, 2017. http://thehill.com/homenews/state-watch/326995-census-more-americans-have-college-degrees-than-ever-before.

Sallie Mae and the Student Debt Crisis (1972-2019)

The massive increases in tuition and other expenses at U.S. colleges and universities since the 1980s forced more and more students to rely upon financial aid to afford higher education. According to the National Center for Education Statistics (2019), 85 percent of full-time undergraduate students received financial aid in academic year 2016-2017. The financial aid available to students can take the form of grants, scholarships, or campus employment, which provide funds that students do not have to repay. However, more than half of student financial aid takes the form of education loans, which students are obligated to repay with interest.

The growing reliance on borrowing to pay rising college costs triggered a student debt crisis in the United States. Surveys indicated that two-thirds of students who earned bachelor's degrees in 2018 owed money for their education, with an average loan balance of $29,200 (Carrns 2019). Debt levels climbed even higher for students who earned postgraduate degrees, one-fourth of whom left school with student loans in excess of $100,000 (Liebenthal 2018). Cumulatively, 45 million Americans owed more than $1.5 trillion in student loan debt in 2018—making it the second-highest source of consumer debt in the United States, behind only home mortgages and ahead of outstanding credit card balances and auto loans (Friedman 2019). For many recent graduates, student loan debt created a financial burden that prevented them from taking vacations, buying homes, saving for retirement, or achieving other goals. As of 2019, more than 5 million Americans were considered to be in default on their student loans, which held negative consequences for their credit ratings and employment prospects (Friedman 2019).

Some critics claimed that U.S. government policies caused and perpetuated the student loan crisis. Beginning with its establishment of the Student Loan Marketing Association (SLMA or Sallie Mae) as a government-sponsored entity (GSE) in 1972, the federal government encouraged students to borrow money to pay for college. Lawmakers thus launched an era in which the financial burden of higher education—which had long been viewed as a public benefit that promoted technological innovation and economic growth—shifted from the larger society to individual students. "I do not accept the notion that the federal government has an obligation to fund generous grants to anybody that wants to go to college," said David Stockman, who served as budget director to President Ronald Reagan. "If people want to go to college bad enough, then there is opportunity and responsibility on their part to finance their way through the best way they can" (Zaloom 2019, 12).

Over the next four decades, as Sallie Mae transitioned from a GSE to a private, for-profit business enterprise, both college costs and student loan debt skyrocketed. Meanwhile, Sallie Mae and other major players in the student loan industry earned massive profits and lobbied the federal government for increasingly favorable treatment. Critics charged that the student loan industry grew at the expense of the nation's college graduates. "An industry that was virtually nonexistent in decades past has grown to dominate the lives of millions of educated Americans," consumer advocate Alan Michael Collinge wrote in *The Student Loan Scam*. "At the same time as student debt grew, most standard consumer protections were removed from this type of debt, with the result that today, student loans have a stranglehold on millions of lower- and middle-class citizens" (Collinge 2009, 1).

In the twenty-first century, the student debt crisis posed difficult challenges for U.S. lawmakers, who sought ways to make higher education more affordable and ease the financial burdens on recent college graduates. "At a time when a higher education has never been more important or more expensive, too many students are facing a choice that they should never have to make," former president Barack Obama stated at a State University of New York at Buffalo commencement ceremony. "Either they say no to college … or you do what it takes to go to college, but then you run the risk that you won't be able to pay it off because you've got so much debt. Now, that's a choice we shouldn't accept. And, by the way, that's a choice that previous generations did not have to accept" (Craig 2015, 18).

Growth of the Student Loan Industry

The federal government first became involved in financing higher education following World War II, when the G.I. Bill provided funding for more than 7 million military veterans to attend college. Federal support for higher education continued during the Cold War, when lawmakers recognized the need to train scientists and engineers to help the United States compete militarily and technologically with the Soviet Union. President Lyndon B. Johnson made education a centerpiece of his Great Society initiatives to help alleviate poverty and eliminate racial injustice. Upon signing the Higher Education Act (HEA) of 1965, which established a system of federal grants, scholarships, and loans designed to increase access to postsecondary education, Johnson asserted that "it is the obligation of your nation to provide and permit and assist every child born in these borders to receive all the education that he can take" (Liebenthal 2019).

The HEA created the Federal Family Education Loan (FFEL) program, through which the federal government provided subsidies and guarantees to encourage private, commercial lenders to issue education loans to students. Since students tended to be young and had limited credit histories, banks considered such loans relatively risky. Although the lenders financed the loans with private capital, government subsidies helped them reduce interest rates and cover expenses. In addition, federal loan guarantees limited the risk to lenders by reimbursing them in case of default. The loans issued under the FFEL program included subsidized and unsubsidized Stafford loans, PLUS loans for parents and graduate students, and consolidation loans. As demand for higher education grew, President Richard M. Nixon expanded the federal Pell Grant program for low-income students. He also created Sallie Mae as a quasi-governmental agency—funded and overseen by the U.S. Department of the Treasury—to purchase student loans from private FFEL lenders. Sallie Mae thus created a secondary market for these government-backed loans, which freed up funds to enable banks to issue more student loans.

By providing funding for higher education, the HEA facilitated a 67 percent increase in the number of American adults who held a four-year college degree within a decade of its passage (Collinge 2009, 3). Yet it also precipitated the student debt crisis by encouraging students to rely upon borrowing to pay for college—and by creating a lucrative business opportunity for lenders, servicers, guarantee agencies, collection agencies, and other private entities involved in the rapidly growing student loan industry. Sallie Mae, in particular, benefitted from its close connection to the federal government. During the 1980s, as college tuition rates began rising at more than twice the rate of inflation, Sallie Mae's assets grew from $1.6 billion to $28.6 billion (Loonin 2014).

The HEA underwent eight reauthorizations and several amendments and extensions over the years. As the student loan financing industry grew more profitable, it used its resources to shape the legislation in its favor. According to consumer advocates, industry lobbyists secured changes that eliminated basic protections for borrowers and gave lenders unprecedented collection powers. For instance, the HEA originally allowed borrowers to discharge federally guaranteed student loan obligations after five years if they experienced undue financial hardship or declared bankruptcy. The 1990 HEA reauthorization extended the time for borrowers to become eligible for discharge to seven years, and in 1998 lawmakers removed bankruptcy protections entirely—making student loans the only type of consumer debt to be nondischargeable in bankruptcy. In 2005, the industry convinced Congress to eliminate bankruptcy protections from private student loans as well as federally guaranteed student loans.

Other amendments to the HEA allowed the student loan financing industry to charge massive penalties and fees for late or missed payments and to use aggressive collection methods against borrowers, such as garnishing wages, seizing income tax refunds, withholding Social Security and disability payments, suspending state-issued professional licenses, and terminating government employment. Industry lobbyists also successfully eliminated statutes of limitations on student loans, enabling collection agencies to go after borrowers who left college decades earlier, and removed provisions allowing student borrowers to refinance their loans at better rates with new lenders. These changes led to tremendous profits for the student loan industry at the expense of student borrowers, who often faced interest, fees, penalties, and collection charges that doubled their original loan balance. In fact, Sallie Mae and other companies earned more money from students who defaulted on their loans than from students who paid their debts in a timely manner. "The corporate lawyers who conceived this self-enriching system ought to get the nation's top prize for shameless perversity," consumer advocate Ralph Nader declared (Collinge 2009, 5).

Sallie Mae Goes Private

In response to complaints about lenders making excessive profits on student loans at the expense of borrowers and taxpayers, President Bill Clinton introduced the Federal Direct Loan Program in 1993. This program enabled the federal government to issue education loans directly to students, cutting out the private banks serving as middlemen. Clinton pointed to studies showing that direct loans offered cost savings to both student borrowers and the federal government. Within two years, federal direct loans accounted for one-third of all student loans issued. As a result, Sallie Mae saw its market value cut in half. In 1994, when Republicans took control of Congress, Sallie Mae successfully lobbied to change its status from a government-sponsored enterprise to a private-sector business, meaning the company would no longer be subject to direct federal oversight and control.

In a series of steps taken over the next decade, Sallie Mae moved toward independent operation while also taking advantage of its federal ties and name recognition to expand its reach in the student loan financing industry. Sallie Mae acquired companies involved in all aspects of education loans, including originators, guarantee agencies, lenders, loan servicers, debt management companies, and collection agencies. By the time the GSE ceased to exist in 2004, Sallie Mae remained a major servicer of federal student loans and also ranked as the nation's leading provider of private student loans, which typically carried much higher interest rates than federal direct loans. As a result of its market dominance, the company's stock price increased by nearly 2,000 percent between 1995 and 2005 (Schorn 2006). Sallie Mae's chief executive officer, Albert Lord, earned more than $200 million during this period (Loonin 2014).

Both during and after the privatization, some aspects of Sallie Mae's business strategies and tactics raised concerns among consumer advocates and federal regulators. According to critics, Sallie Mae worked to undermine the Federal Direct Loan program by paying colleges and universities to steer student borrowers toward its private loans instead. The company offered perks to financial aid officers—including lavish dinner parties, golf outings, free tickets to concerts and sporting events, and all-expenses-paid resort vacations—to become the "preferred lender" for their universities. Sallie Mae also established incentive programs that allowed colleges to keep a percentage of each student loan they routed through the company. In some cases, Sallie Mae provided employees to answer telephones in university financial aid offices and give students advice about student loans. These efforts helped limit federal direct loans to 19 percent of the market by 2006 (Collinge 2009, 12), while Sallie Mae's loan holdings grew to reach $123 billion that year—up from $45 billion a decade earlier (Collinge 2009, 23). In 2007, a legal settlement forced Sallie Mae to stop these practices and pay $2 million to educate students about the risks and benefits of using loans to pay for college.

Sallie Mae also used its financial power and government connections to lobby for legislative changes that gave special advantages to the student loan industry. From 2007 to 2013, the company and its executives donated more than $22.7 million to congressional campaigns and political action committees (Loonin 2014). In a letter to the U.S. Departments of Education and Treasury, Senator Elizabeth Warren (D-MA) asserted that Sallie Mae received many unfair benefits in exchange, such as lucrative contracts to service federal student loans, opportunities to borrow money at extremely low interest rates, and profits of over $600 million from selling federal student loans back to the government (Loonin 2014). "Given a for-profit company's imperative to do what is best for its investors, it is especially critical that the government conduct rigorous oversight of its private contractors," wrote Deanne Loonin of the National Consumer Law Center. "Unfortunately, the growing number of government investigations and consumer complaints show that government supervision has been lax at best" (Loonin 2014).

Reform of the Student Loan System

In 2009, President Barack Obama announced his intention to end the FFEL program and transition to the Federal Direct Loan program for all government-backed student loans. "We have a student loan system where we're giving lenders billions of dollars in wasteful subsidies that could be used to make college more affordable for all Americans," he stated. "Under the FFEL program, taxpayers are paying banks a premium to act as middle-men—a premium that costs the American people billions of dollars each year. Well, that's a premium we cannot afford—not when we could be reinvesting that same money in our students, in our economy, and in our country" (Obama 2009). Obama estimated that this change would save taxpayers between $6 billion and $8 billion per year for ten years, which would pay for new federal grants designed to make college more affordable for millions of students. Although Sallie Mae and other companies involved in the student loan industry objected to Obama's plan, the Democratic-controlled Congress ended the FFEL program in 2010 with the passage of the Student Aid and Fiscal Responsibility Act.

Although federal direct loans offered student borrowers lower interest rates and more flexible repayment options than private loans, both college costs and student loan debt continued to increase over the next decade. In 2014, Sallie Mae divided its business interests into two separate entities: Navient Corporation, a publicly traded company that acted as a servicer and collector of federal student loans; and Sallie Mae Bank, a lender that offered private student loans. Consumer advocates claimed that Navient and other student loan servicers engaged in deceptive, exploitive, and predatory business practices that harmed student borrowers. Navient faced numerous lawsuits from the Consumer Financial Protection Bureau and state attorneys general accusing the company of misleading borrowers in order to extract interest, fees, and penalties. Navient executives described the allegations as false and vowed to defend the company's practices in court. Meanwhile, Sallie Mae received negative news coverage in 2019 for taking 100 executives and sales team members to Hawaii for an all-expenses-paid resort vacation to celebrate a record year in which the company issued $5 billion in private student loans to 374,000 borrowers (Beck, Pou, and Kesslen 2019).

The student debt crisis weighed heavily on a generation of Americans who struggled for years to repay the loans they used to finance their education. "The new American dream is strikingly minimalist," Ephrat Livni wrote for Quartz. "Today, many Americans in their 20s, 30s, and 40s consider themselves lucky so long as they have a job that allows them to make their student loan payments. For the 44 million who bet on themselves, borrowed money to study, and currently owe on those loans, their decisions and ambitions are shaped by the burden of early debt" (Livni 2018). The prospect of taking on significant student debt led many Americans to question the value of a college education. In a 2018 Pew Research survey of young professionals with student debt, only 46 percent said that the benefits of higher education outweighed the costs. In addition, the respondents were twice as likely to report struggling financially as young people without student debt (Cilluffo 2019). As the student debt crisis increasingly threatened to harm the U.S. economy, lawmakers proposed various reforms intended to bring relief to student borrowers, ranging from forgiving all federal student loans to restoring refinancing rights and other basic consumer protections.

Further Reading

Beck, Catie, Jackeline Pou, and Ben Kesslen. 2019. "Sallie Mae Execs Tan at Maui Retreat While Student Debt Crisis Tops $1.6 Trillion." NBC News, October 17, 2019. https://www.nbcnews.com/news/us-news/sallie-mae-execs-tan-maui-retreat-while-student-debt-crisis-n1063826.

Carrns, Ann. 2019. "Two-Thirds of College Students Take On Debt, but Amount Is Rising More Slowly." *New York Times*, September 27 2019. https://www.nytimes.com/2019/09/27/your-money/student-debt-what-to-do.html.

Cilluffo, Anthony. 2019. "Five Facts about Student Loans." Pew Research Center, August 13, 2019. https://www.pewresearch.org/fact-tank/2019/08/13/facts-about-student-loans/.

Collinge, Alan Michael. 2009. *The Student Loan Scam: The Most Oppressive Debt in U.S. History—and How We Can Fight Back*. Boston: Beacon Press, 2009.

Craig, Ryan. 2015. *College Disrupted: The Great Unbundling of Higher Education*. New York: St. Martin's Press.

Friedman, Zach. 2019. "Student Loan Debt Statistics in 2019: A $1.5 Trillion Crisis." *Forbes*, February 25, 2019. https://www.forbes.com/sites/zackfriedman/2019/02/25/student-loan-debt-statistics-2019/#3bb42199133f.

Hsu, Hua. 2019. "Student Debt Is Transforming the American Family." *New Yorker*, September 9, 2019. https://www.newyorker.com/magazine/2019/09/09/student-debt-is-transforming-the-american-family.

Liebenthal, Ryann. 2018. "Unforgivable: The Incredible, Rage-Inducing Inside Story of America's Student Debt Machine." *Mother Jones*, September/October 2018. https://www.motherjones.com/politics/2018/08/debt-student-loan-forgiveness-betsy-devos-education-department-fedloan/.

Livni, Ephrat. 2018. "$1.5 Trillion of Student Loan Debt Has Transformed the American Dream." Quartz, August 24, 2018. https://qz.com/1367412/1-5-trillion-of-us-student-loan-debt-has-transformed-the-american-dream/.

Loonin, Deanne. 2014. "The Sallie Mae Saga: A Government-Created, Student-Debt Fueled Profit Machine." National Consumer Law Center, January 2014. https://www.studentloanborrowerassistance.org/wp-content/uploads/File/report-sallie-mae-saga.pdf.

National Center for Education Statistics. 2019. "Sources of Financial Aid." Institute of Education Sciences, May 2019. https://nces.ed.gov/programs/coe/indicator_cuc.asp.

Obama, Barack. 2009. "Remarks by the President on Higher Education." White House, April 24, 2009. https://web.archive.org/web/20150209030340/https://www.whitehouse.gov/the_press_office/Remarks-by-the-President-on-Higher-Education/.

Schorn, Daniel. 2006. "Sallie Mae's Success Too Costly?" *60 Minutes,* CBS News, May 5, 2006. https://www.cbsnews.com/news/sallie-maes-success-too-costly/5/.

Zaloom, Caitlin. 2019. *Indebted: How Families Make College Work at Any Cost.* Princeton, NJ: Princeton University Press.

The Public Service Loan Forgiveness Program (2007)

Recognizing the value of higher education to society, the U.S. government established numerous programs over the years to help citizens afford to go to college. Some of these programs aimed to increase access to education for specific groups, such as military veterans or students from low-income families. Other programs offered financial incentives for students to pursue certain areas of study, such as medicine or engineering, in order to address societal needs. The main forms of federal student aid included grants, loans, and work-study employment opportunities.

In 2007, Congress established the Public Service Loan Forgiveness (PSLF) program. It encouraged college graduates to work in public-service jobs—such as public safety, public health, education, nonprofit administration, and government service—by offering to cancel the outstanding balance of their federal student loans after 10 years of qualifying payments. The PSLF program effectively rewarded graduates for filling public-sector professions, which often required advanced education credentials yet paid around 25 percent less than equivalent private-sector positions (Liebenthal 2018).

By 2017, when the first cohort of students became eligible for loan cancellation, several federal agencies and watchdog groups raised concerns about the PSLF program. Critics pointed out that the U.S. Department of

Education rejected 99 percent of all applications for loan forgiveness submitted through the program, leaving borrowers to question life decisions they made in an effort to qualify. After reviewing thousands of borrower complaints about the PSLF, Seth Frotman—the head of the Consumer Financial Protection Bureau's student loan office—resigned in disgust, accusing the Donald Trump administration of putting the profits of large financial services companies above the interests of ordinary Americans.

Debt Relief for Public Service

Congress established the PSLF program under the College Cost Reduction and Access Act (CCRAA), which received bipartisan support. Upon signing the measure into law on September 27, 2007, President George W. Bush declared that it would "help millions of low-income Americans earn a college degree" (Bush 2007). The CCRAA amended the Higher Education Act of 1965 by extending need-based federal Pell Grants through 2017 and authorizing a gradual increase in the maximum Pell Grant amount from $4,300 to $5,400 per year. The new law also eliminated a provision that tied students' Pell Grant awards to their tuition bills. This "tuition sensitivity" provision came under criticism for penalizing low-income students who chose to attend cost-effective institutions of higher learning.

The CCRAA also introduced a 50 percent reduction in interest rates on government-subsidized Stafford Loans, from 6.8 percent prior to July 2008 to 3.4 percent by July 2011. In an effort to address rising levels of student loan debt, the legislation also created an Income-Based Repayment (IBR) plan for federal loans. IBR capped student borrowers' maximum monthly loan payments at 15 percent of their discretionary income—defined as the amount by which their annual adjusted gross income exceeded 150 percent of the federal poverty line for their family size—and canceled any remaining loan balance after 25 years. When the program took effect in 2009, the federal poverty line stood at $10,830 for an individual or $22,050 for a family of four. Under IBR, therefore, only income above $16,245 for an individual or $33,075 for a family of four counted toward determining the amount of monthly student loan payments. Borrowers who earned less were not required to make payments.

The CCRAA also established the Public Service Loan Forgiveness Program with the goal of rewarding college graduates who pursued public-service careers rather than accepting more lucrative private-sector jobs. Lawmakers recognized that the prospect of paying back mountains of student debt pushed many graduates toward high-income career options, even if they had a real interest in community service. Fewer law school graduates were willing to serve as public defenders, for instance, when working for a big corporate law firm seemed necessary to repay their student loans. The PSLF program made public-service jobs more appealing by offering to cancel the remaining student loan balance for borrowers who worked full-time in the public sector and made 120 qualifying payments.

Congress estimated the total cost of debt relief and other education benefits provided under the CCRAA at around $20 billion. The legislation covered most of its own costs by eliminating federal subsidies for private lenders and guarantee agencies that handled student loans. Critics charged that financial services companies used government subsidies to increase profits for their executives and shareholders at the expense of taxpayers and student borrowers. In the face of opposition from lenders, however, the Department of Education contracted with some of these same companies to "service" federal student loans. Servicers handled the day-to-day work of dealing with 40 million student borrowers, such as answering questions, explaining options, doing paperwork, keeping records, managing accounts, and collecting payments.

The Consumer Financial Protection Bureau

Shortly after the passage of the CCRAA, a global financial crisis sent the U.S. economy spiraling into a severe recession. Critics called for increased federal regulation of the financial services industry, blaming high-risk business practices by Wall Street banks and investment firms for the hardships affecting the American people. Congress responded by passing the Dodd-Frank Wall Street Reform and Consumer Protection Act, which President Barack Obama signed into law in 2010. Dodd-Frank created the Consumer Financial Protection Bureau (CFPB), a federal agency tasked with helping consumers make informed financial decisions and protecting them from abusive practices by the financial services industry. The legislation also established an independent student loan ombudsman within the CFPB to focus on protecting the interests of student borrowers.

From its creation in 2011 through 2017, the office of the CFPB student loan ombudsman reviewed more than 60,000 consumer complaints and returned more than $750 million to student borrowers it determined to have been deceived or treated unfairly by lenders, servicers, or debt collectors (Turner 2018b). CFPB and several state attorneys general filed lawsuits against large loan servicers like Navient (formerly Sallie Mae), for example, accusing the company of misleading borrowers, processing payments incorrectly, failing to respond to complaints, and overcharging interest and fees. Navient chief executive officer Jack Remondi released a statement calling the charges "unfounded" and claiming that "the lawsuit is another attempt to blame a single servicer for the failures of the higher education system and the federal student loan program to deliver desired outcomes" (Turner 2018b).

Attorney Seth Frotman joined the CFPB at its inception and assumed the position of student loan ombudsman in 2016. He immediately launched an investigation into servicers' handling of the PSLF program, which was the source of thousands of consumer complaints. In June 2017, the CFPB issued a report warning that a pattern of mistakes and mismanagement by loan servicers threatened to derail the program. Frotman noted that most borrowers who attempted to invoke their rights to loan forgiveness under PSLF encountered "a range of student loan industry practices that delay, defer, or deny access to expected debt relief" (Frotman 2017).

Thousands of librarians, social workers, police officers, teachers, nurses, and other public-service professionals who planned to take advantage of the PSLF program contacted the CFPB about problems they experienced in dealing with loan servicing contractors, such as FedLoan. Some servicers knew of borrowers' public-service employment but never told them about the PSLF program. Some servicers failed to file required paperwork or complete basic steps necessary for borrowers to qualify for PSLF. Some borrowers notified loan servicers of their intention to enroll in PSLF, double-checked to ensure their eligibility, and made the required on-time payments for years, only to be informed that they used the wrong repayment system and thus did not qualify for loan cancellation.

Although Frotman's report recommended several changes to improve administration of the PSLF program, the Department of Education did not take action. Six months later, in October 2017, the first cohort of borrowers became eligible to apply for student loan forgiveness under the program. Within the next year, the Department of Education processed 29,000 PSLF applications and rejected 99 percent of them for "not meeting program requirements" (Turner 2018b). This dismal figure led to an investigation by the Government Accounting Office (GAO), which blamed poor communication between the Department of Education and private loan servicers for creating confusion about PSLF requirements. For instance, FedLoan claimed that it could not assess borrowers' eligibility for PSLF because it never received a list of qualified public-service employers. The Department of Education, in turn, blamed Congress for enacting overly strict rules for PSLF eligibility.

Congress responded to the complaints about PSLF by providing a new opportunity for borrowers to qualify called the Temporary Expanded Public Service Loan Forgiveness Program (TEPSLF). Public-service workers whose applications for student loan cancellation were denied under the original program because they participated in the wrong repayment plan could reapply for debt relief under the new program. TEPSLF did not improve the situation for borrowers, however. By the end of 2019, the Department of Education had only approved 2,246 applications out of 161,328 submitted—a rejection rate of 98.6 percent (Swaminathan 2020).

In the meantime, Frotman and other officials in the CFPB's student loan office grew increasingly frustrated with the Trump administration, which they felt actively undermined their ability to protect student borrowers from misinformation, mistakes, and mismanagement by loan servicers. In November 2017, Trump installed former U.S. Representative Mick Mulvaney (R-SC) as acting director of the CFPB. Mulvaney criticized the agency during his tenure in Congress—calling it "a joke … in a sick, sad kind of way" (Turner 2018a)—and as director took steps to reduce its regulatory and enforcement powers. For instance, he reorganized the student loan office and placed it within the financial education section, thus shifting its emphasis from consumer protection to consumer information. Trump's secretary of education, Betsy DeVos, announced that her department would no longer share student loan data with the CFPB, describing the agency as "overreaching and unaccountable" (Turner 2018a). In addition, DeVos moved to protect student loan servicers from state-level oversight, arguing that private contractors working for the federal government were immune from lawsuits brought by state attorneys general.

In August 2018, Frotman resigned from his position as CFPB student loan ombudsman. He outlined his reasons for quitting in a scathing letter addressed to Mulvaney. "You have used the bureau to serve the wishes of the most powerful financial companies in America," he wrote. "The damage you have done to the bureau betrays these families and sacrifices the financial futures of millions of Americans in communities across the country" (Associated Press 2018). Frotman's resignation received national news coverage and led to congressional hearings on the federal government's handling of the student debt crisis. In March 2019, Frotman testified before the House Financial Services Committee and asked its members for strong legislation to protect student borrowers. "We cannot continue to treat student loan borrowers as second-class citizens simply because the word 'student' comes before the word 'loan.' Student loan borrowers face breakdowns and harmful practices that we would simply never permit in other markets," he stated. "Right now, we have a trillion-dollar black hole in our financial markets. Millions of Americans with student debt are falling further behind as their federal government coddles predatory players" (Frotman 2019).

In its 2021 budget proposal, the Trump administration suggested eliminating the PSLF program and replacing it with an income-based repayment plan that provided for loan forgiveness after 15 years. "Our proposal is to sunset the public service loan forgiveness program," DeVos explained. "The administration feels that incentivizing one type of work and one type of job over another is not called for" (Swaminathan 2020). In contrast, several 2020 Democratic presidential candidates proposed broad plans to cancel most outstanding student loan debt. Senator Elizabeth Warren (D-MA), whose work led to the formation of the CFPB, promised to forgive $50,000 in student loans for borrowers with household income under $100,000, which meant full cancellation for 75 percent of all borrowers.

Further Reading

Associated Press. 2018. "Top U.S. Student Loans Official Resigns over 'Open Hostility' from White House." *Guardian,* August 27, 2018. https://www.theguardian.com/us-news/2018/aug/27/seth-frotman-student-loan-ombudsman-resigns-white-house-hostility.

Bush, George W. 2007. "President Bush Signs the College Cost Reduction and Access Act." White House, September 27, 2007. https://georgewbush-whitehouse.archives.gov/news/releases/2007/09/20070927-3.html.

Frotman, Seth. 2017. "Staying on Track While Giving Back." Consumer Financial Protection Bureau, June 2017. https://files.consumerfinance.gov/f/documents/201706_cfpb_PSLF-midyear-report.pdf.

Frotman, Seth. 2019. "Testimony before the United States Congress House Financial Services Committee." Student Borrower Protection Center, March 7, 2019. https://financialservices.house.gov/uploadedfiles/hhrg-116-ba00-wstate-frotmans-20190307.pdf.

Liebenthal, Ryann. 2018. "Unforgivable: The Incredible, Rage-Inducing Inside Story of America's Student Debt Machine." *Mother Jones,* September/October 2018. https://www.motherjones.com/politics/2018/08/debt-student-loan-forgiveness-betsy-devos-education-department-fedloan/.

Stewart, Emily. 2019. "Elizabeth Warren Has Just One Plan." Vox, September 20, 2019. https://www.vox.com/policy-and-politics/2019/9/20/20867899/elizabeth-warren-cfpb-founding-plans-obama-president.

Swaminathan, Aarthi. 2020. "Trump Administration Plan to Sunset the Public Service Loan Forgiveness Program Would Be 'Devastating,' Expert Says." Yahoo! Finance, March 7, 2020. https://finance.yahoo.com/news/pslf-program-sunset-student-loans-135004757.html.

Turner, Cory. 2018a. "Student Loan Watchdog Quits, Says Trump Administration 'Turned Its Back' on Borrowers." NPR, August 27, 2018. https://www.npr.org/2018/08/27/642199524/student-loan-watchdog-quits-blames-trump-administration.

Turner, Cory. 2018b. "Why Public Service Loan Forgiveness Is So Unforgiving."
    NPR, October 17, 2018. https://www.npr.org/2018/10/17/653853227/
    the-student-loan-whistleblower.

For-Profit College Scams (2008-2018)

During the 2017-2018 academic year, higher education in the United
States encompassed academic instruction or career training delivered
through nearly 6,000 institutions nationwide. According to the National
Center for Education Statistics (2019), around half of these institutions
operated on a not-for-profit basis, including 1,586 public universities and
community colleges funded primarily through state and local appropriations, as well as 1,397 private colleges funded primarily through tuition,
charitable contributions, or religious affiliations. The other half operated
as profit-seeking, commercial business ventures, including 900 degree-
granting schools and nearly 2,000 non-degree-granting institutions offering
proprietary vocational or technical training programs designed to prepare
students for specific careers.

The for-profit college sector emerged in 1972, when an amendment to
the Higher Education Act routed Title IV federal financial aid funds directly
to students rather than to institutions. Lawmakers intended for this change
to increase access to higher education for nontraditional students from marginalized groups, including students of color, first-generation college students, students from low-income families, and students with disabilities.
For-profit institutions appealed to these students by offering practical,
skill-based, occupational training in specific, high-demand employment
fields, such as construction, health care, or culinary arts. For-profit schools
also offered flexible class schedules and ranked among the earliest adopters
of online learning, making it easier for students to balance education with
full-time work. The for-profit sector expanded over the years, and total
enrollment grew from around 230,000 students in the 1990s to reach a
record high of 2 million in 2010 (Associated Press 2017).

A number of for-profit colleges came under scrutiny for their business
practices, however, which led to fraud investigations and calls for stronger
federal oversight of the industry. Critics charged that for-profit colleges
used deceptive recruiting practices to prey upon vulnerable populations
and increase enrollment. These schools failed to deliver quality instruction,
according to critics, and many students either dropped out or received useless degrees that did not improve their employment opportunities. Since
most students depended on federal financial aid to pay tuition, for-profit

schools essentially earned revenue at the expense of taxpayers while producing poor educational and employment outcomes. "These for-profits rely almost exclusively on federal student loans and cost significantly more than public institutions. Many are owned by hedge funds or are publicly traded," said Kentucky Attorney General Jack Conway. "Not all for-profit schools are bad, but too many abuse the public trust by showing greater interest in profiting from student loan money than educating students" (Conway 2011). Critics also pointed out that students who attended for-profit colleges had the highest default rates on education loans, thus exacerbating the student debt crisis in the United States.

Under President Barack Obama, the federal government exposed and cracked down on some of the abuses of the for-profit college industry. The administration enacted new regulations that restricted college recruiting practices, set standards for graduates' employment outcomes, and provided for student loan forgiveness in cases of fraud. The negative publicity surrounding the industry led to steep declines in enrollment, which combined with the withdrawal of federal funding to cause the closure of 40 percent of the for-profit colleges that existed in 2010 (Dayen 2019). Upon taking office in 2017, however, President Donald Trump—who once operated his own for-profit college, Trump University—rescinded many of the Obama-era regulations that offered fraud protection for students at for-profit schools.

Shady Practices at For-Profit Colleges

The nonprofit model of higher education developed partly as a way to focus institutional resources on the educational mission. Whether nonprofit colleges and universities received most of their funding from public sources, private endowments, or tuition payments, they reinvested their income in facilities and instruction for the benefit of students. For-profit schools, on the other hand, operated as businesses with an imperative to generate profits for investors. Some critics argued that the profit motive conflicted with the educational mission, because any money spent on students reduced the financial returns for owners, investors, and executives. "Why does the for-profit sector generate these terrible outcomes?" said Barmak Nassirian of the American Association of State Colleges and Universities. "Because terrible outcomes are very profitable, and there are no adverse consequences visited upon corporations that generate absolutely abysmal consequences, for both students and the taxpayers" (Simon 2018).

For-profit institutions of higher education depended on tuition payments as their primary sources of income, which placed a premium on student enrollment. Critics accused many for-profit schools of using aggressive, predatory marketing strategies and recruitment methods to lure new students. Some for-profit colleges advertised extensively on television, websites, billboards, and public transportation. Others used professional "lead generators" to identify potential students who met certain demographic criteria. In 2012, a lead-generator company called QuinStreet paid $2.5 million to settle claims that it falsely presented itself as a government-affiliated informational website in order to mislead veterans about educational options and steer them to for-profit colleges (Perez 2012). A two-year investigation by the U.S. Senate Committee on Health, Education, Labor, and Pensions (HELP) found that for-profit colleges devoted a significant amount of their total revenue to non-education-related expenses. In 2009, for instance, the industry spent 22.7 percent of revenue on advertising, recruiting, and admissions, compared to 17.2 percent on curriculum and instruction (HELP 2012).

In many cases, for-profit education companies targeted working adults, people of color, women, veterans, and first-generation college students. Recruiters often pursued these candidates relentlessly, using tactics designed to expose and take advantage of their feelings of insecurity and vulnerability. In a series of interviews for the documentary film *Fail State,* students reported "being harassed with phone calls, emotionally manipulated, deceived about costs, and persuaded that their post-secondary educations would land them implausibly high-paying jobs" (Nevins 2018). In 2015, the U.S. Department of Education fined one of the largest for-profit education providers, Corinthian Colleges, $30 million for inflating graduates' job placement and salary data in its recruiting materials. Corinthian eventually shut down 28 college campuses, leaving 16,000 students stranded partway through degree programs (Johnson 2015).

Betsy DeVos, who became secretary of education in the Trump administration in 2017, argued that consumers had a responsibility to research their college options and make informed decisions. "Students should go into higher education with their eyes wide open," she stated (Flannery 2018). Yet critics charged that for-profit schools intentionally targeted individuals who lacked the experience and resources to evaluate their claims and were thus most likely to succumb to deceptive, high-pressure sales tactics. Internal documents showed that Corinthian Colleges specifically pursued single mothers subsisting near the federal poverty line, for instance, as well as people who experienced low self-esteem and social isolation (Nevins 2018). "Students from low income communities who don't have a tradition of college-going in their family," said education researcher Stephanie Cellini, "are they able to assess the quality of these schools, especially if there's strong advertising and heavy recruitment and sometimes false promises?" (Simon 2018).

The student demographic targeted by for-profit colleges tended to be eligible for need-based federal financial aid under Title IV of the Higher Education Act. In many cases, for-profit education companies encouraged students to take out student loans to cover their tuition. According to the HELP committee report, 96 percent of students at for-profit schools financed their education with student loans, compared to 13 percent at community colleges, 48 percent at public universities, and 57 percent at private colleges. As a result, the HELP committee investigation revealed that the for-profit college industry received $32 billion in federal funds during the 2009-2010 academic year. This amount represented about one-fourth of all student aid disbursed by the U.S. Department of Education, even though for-profit schools accounted for only 13 percent of total college enrollment. Corinthian Colleges alone collected $1.4 billion per year in federal student aid funds (Nevins 2018). For some for-profit colleges, federal student aid money provided more than 80 percent of total funding.

Even adjusting for differences in socioeconomic backgrounds, for-profit college students experienced worse educational outcomes than nonprofit college students. The HELP committee investigation found that more than half of all students who enrolled in for-profit colleges in 2008-2009 dropped out without earning a degree or diploma—with an average length of attendance of four months—only to learn that any credits they earned would not transfer to nonprofit schools. Furthermore, for-profit college students were less likely to find employment upon graduation and earned lower average salaries than their peers at nonprofit colleges. These poor outcomes, coupled with high levels of borrowing, meant that many for-profit college students struggled to pay their student loans. "The people who are being affected and preyed upon by these schools are some of the most voiceless in our society, and their arcs are very similar," noted documentary filmmaker Alex Shebanow. "They were promised the world. It was affordable. You don't need to worry about your student loan debt. And they enrolled and realized their education was leading nowhere, or some realized the scam halfway through and dropped out, but had all this debt they'd taken on" (Nevins 2018).

Cracking Down on For-Profit Abuses

Critics called for greater oversight of the for-profit education industry, arguing that the federal government should hold for-profit education companies accountable for collecting huge amounts of student aid funding while failing to produce value for students or taxpayers. "We need to be really cautious," Cellini said. "I think the profit motive can sometimes get in the way of the best interests of students, so I do think regulation and oversight is needed" (Simon 2018). As the student debt crisis emerged as a major economic issue, the HELP report revealed that for-profit school attendees accounted for nearly half of all defaults on student loans (HELP 2012). Growing numbers of student complaints brought negative media attention to for-profit schools as well as fraud investigations by state attorneys general.

Upon taking office in 2009, Obama enacted or enforced a series of regulations aimed at protecting students in the for-profit education sector from predatory or fraudulent business practices. For instance, the U.S. Department of Education made it illegal for institutions of higher learning to offer incentives to recruiters based on the number of students they convinced to enroll. The department also required schools that offered online courses to provide "substantive teacher-student interaction." Obama also instituted the "90-10" rule, which required for-profit schools to receive at least 10 percent of their funding from sources other than student financial aid. In addition, the administration implemented the "gainful employment" rule, which withdrew federal funding from poor-performing schools whose graduates failed to achieve specific debt-to-earnings ratios. Finally, the Department of Education enacted "borrower defense" regulations, which allowed students to file claims for federal loan forgiveness if they had been defrauded by institutions of higher learning. The Obama administration approved $655 million in student loan cancellations under this program (AP 2017).

The new regulations—along with the withdrawal of federal funding from institutions that violated the rules—put pressure on the for-profit education industry. Negative publicity led to declining enrollment, from the peak of 2 million in 2010 to around 900,000 by 2017 (Flannery 2018). Several large education companies experienced financial distress and went out of business during this period, including Corinthian Colleges, Education Management Corporation, and ITT Technical Institute. After Trump took office in 2017, however, the Department of Education rolled back or eliminated many of the regulations that had been put in place by his predecessor. Critics noted that Trump had operated a for-profit education enterprise called Trump University from 2005 to 2010, which promoted itself as a non-degree program in real estate and wealth management. Trump University closed in the wake of a series of lawsuits accusing the company of using aggressive sales tactics and false promises to defraud students out of thousands of dollars. In 2018, Trump paid $25 million to settle the lawsuits and reimburse students.

DeVos claimed that the Obama administration had targeted for-profit schools unfairly. "For-profit or not-for-profit is simply a matter of tax status," she stated. "Fraud anywhere needs to be rooted out" (AP 2017). Under her leadership, the Department of Education immediately suspended the gainful employment rule and restored federal funding to poor-performing schools. The department also weakened the borrower defense rule and made it more difficult for students victimized by scam colleges to receive loan forgiveness. Student advocate Pauline Abernathy of The Institute for College Access and Success (TICAS) said the Trump administration gave the for-profit college industry "everything they've lobbied for and more" (Flannery 2018).

DeVos also appointed Julian Schmoke Jr.—the former dean of for-profit DeVry University, which in 2016 paid $100 million to settle lawsuits accusing the company of defrauding students for profit—as head of the federal government office charged with investigating for-profit college abuses. Senator Elizabeth Warren (D-MA) expressed outrage at the choice, arguing that "Secretary DeVos has filled the department with for-profit college hacks who only care about making sham schools rich and shutting down investigations into fraud" (Flannery 2018).

As DeVos made these changes, the progressive Century Foundation released a report showing that for-profit schools accounted for nearly all of the fraud complaints lodged with the Department of Education under the borrower protection program. As of June 2018, students had filed more than 127,800 claims seeking federal loan forgiveness on the basis of fraud—an increase of 27 percent from a year earlier. The Century Foundation analysis found that 98.6 percent of these student complaints referenced for-profit colleges, while only 1.4 percent concerned nonprofit schools. DeVry University accounted for the largest increase in fraud claims, from a total of 1,200 complaints in 2017 to nearly 7,400 in 2018 (Simon 2018). The study's authors argued that the "disproportionate concentration of predatory behavior among for-profit colleges" raised "serious concerns about the federal government's current approach to providing relief to students who have been defrauded and misled" (AP 2017).

For-profit education supporters blamed the Obama administration for the increase in borrower defense complaints, arguing that its broad regulations encouraged students to make unsubstantiated claims for loan forgiveness. In 2018, Republicans in Congress introduced the Promoting Real Opportunity, Success, and Prosperity through Education Reform (PROSPER) Act, which proposed turning the regulatory changes initiated by DeVos into law as well as eliminating the 90-10 rule limiting the percent of for-profit college revenues collected from taxpayers. Critics expressed concern that these changes could reverse the fortunes of the for-profit education sector and enable more schools to harm more students. "If for-profit schools don't want to be responsible for borrower defense claims and reimbursing taxpayers, then they could simply not cheat their students," said attorney Toby Merrill of the Project on Predatory Student Lending at Harvard University (AP 2017).

Further Reading

Associated Press. 2017. "For-Profit Colleges Linked to Almost All Loan Fraud Claims." CBS News, November 9, 2017. https://www.cbsnews.com/news/study-most-student-loan-fraud-claims-involve-for-profits/.

Conway, Jack. 2011. "For-Profit Recruiters and the 'Pain Funnel.'" *New York Times,* June 5, 2011. https://www.nytimes.com/roomfordebate/2011/06/05/how-to-regulate-for-profit-colleges/for-profit-recruiters-and-the-pain-funnel.

Dayen, David. 2019. "Betsy DeVos Quietly Making It Easier for Dying For-Profit Schools to Rip Off a Few More Students on the Way Out." *The Intercept,* April 12, 2019. https://theintercept.com/2019/04/12/betsy-devos-for-profit-colleges/.

Flannery, Mary Ellen. 2018. "Despite Widespread Fraud, For-Profit Colleges Get Green Light from DeVos." *NEA Today,* June 1, 2018. http://neatoday.org/2018/06/01/for-profit-colleges-fraud/.

Health, Education, Labor, and Pensions (HELP) Committee. 2012. "For-Profit Higher Education: The Failure to Safeguard the Federal Investment and Ensure Student Success." U.S. Senate, July 30, 2012. https://www.help.senate.gov/imo/media/for_profit_report/PartI-PartIII-SelectedAppendixes.pdf.

Johnson, Alex. 2015. "Corinthian Colleges Shuts Down, Ending Classes for 16,000 Overnight." NBC News, April 26, 2015. https://www.nbcnews.com/news/education/corinthian-colleges-shuts-down-ending-classes-16-000-overnight-n348741.

National Center for Education Statistics. 2019. "Characteristics of Degree-Granting Postsecondary Institutions." Institute of Education Sciences, May 2019. https://nces.ed.gov/programs/coe/indicator_csa.asp.

Nevins, Jake. 2018. "'Phenomenally Saddening': Inside the Sordid World of America's For-Profit Colleges." *Guardian,* November 9, 2018. https://www.theguardian.com/film/2018/nov/09/fail-state-documentary-for-profit-colleges.

Perez, Erica. 2012. "QuinStreet Settles Complaints It Misled Veterans." *SF Gate,* June 28, 2012. https://www.sfgate.com/education/article/QuinStreet-settles-complaints-it-misled-veterans-3671497.php.

Simon, Caroline. 2018. "For-Profit Colleges' Teachable Moment: 'Terrible Outcomes Are Very Profitable.'" *Forbes,* March 19, 2018. https://

www.forbes.com/sites/schoolboard/2018/03/19/for-profit-colleges-teachable-moment-terrible-outcomes-are-very-profitable/#5f58805140f5.

The Occupy Colleges Movement (2011)

In the fall of 2011, anger and frustration about rising college costs, mounting student loan debt, and poor employment prospects led to a series of protests on college campuses across the United States. Student activists with the Occupy Colleges movement walked out of classrooms, organized rallies, and set up encampments on university property. Inspired by the Occupy Wall Street protests against economic inequality in New York City, the student movement spread quickly through social media. "Around the country, more and more high school students are foregoing a college education because their families can no longer afford it. So many more are graduating with inconceivable amounts of debt and stepping into the worst job market in decades," said a statement the Occupy Colleges website. "They take unpaid internships that go nowhere and soon can't pay college loans. We represent students who share these fears and support Occupy Wall Street" (Fairbanks 2011).

Recession Shapes Students' Outlook

The students who participated in the Occupy Colleges protests saw their futures shaped by the global financial crisis and economic recession that struck in 2008, just as they entered the realm of higher education. The federal government approved a $700 billion bailout package to rescue failing investment banks and prevent the collapse of the financial system. Critics charged that the bank bailout placed the burden of large corporations' unsound business practices and investment strategies on American taxpayers, while preventing those responsible for the financial crisis from facing the consequences of their actions. Some attributed the lenient treatment of the financial industry to excessive corporate influence in the U.S. political system.

As the nation gradually recovered from the recession, critics argued that the main benefits of restored economic growth went to wealthy CEOs and stockholders rather than to working people, thus exacerbating the problem of income inequality in the United States. From 2009 to 2012, for instance, the annual incomes of the top 1 percent of earners increased by 30 percent, while those of the bottom 99 percent grew by only 0.5 percent. By 2015, the top 1 percent of American families earned an average of 26 times more income per year than the other 99 percent of families (Reinicke 2018).

In September 2011, activists with the Occupy Wall Street movement organized a series of grassroots protests in New York City that quickly spread across the country. The protesters occupied Zuccotti Park in Manhattan's financial district for two months before police forced them to disperse. Using the slogan "We Are the 99 Percent," Occupy Wall Street supporters called attention to extreme disparities in the distribution of wealth in the United States. Their demands included an end to government corruption and corporate greed, an overhaul of the financial system, a higher minimum wage, and forgiveness of all student debt. Although critics derided the Occupy protests as disorganized and violent, many prominent figures praised them for bringing the problem of economic inequality into public discourse. "I think it expresses the frustrations the American people feel," said President Barack Obama. "We had the biggest financial crisis since the Great Depression, huge collateral damage all throughout the country" (Memoli 2011).

The issues raised by the Occupy Wall Street movement resonated strongly with many college students, who faced a future of economic insecurity due to rising tuition costs, huge student loan burdens, and dismal job prospects. "There's this broad sense of alienation among this generation, both in terms of how they're going to get jobs and where the direction of the nation is headed," said Columbia University professor Shamus Khan. "They don't feel secure in the world they're about to inherit" (Fairbanks and Knafo 2011). A group of college students and recent graduates in Los Angeles organized a grassroots spinoff movement, Occupy Colleges, and promoted it on social media. The concept received more than 7,000 "likes" on Facebook within a few days, and fellow students began forming chapters at universities across the country.

Student Protests on College Campuses

On October 5, 2011, activists affiliated with Occupy Colleges walked out of class at an estimated 100 institutions nationwide to express solidarity with Occupy Wall Street as well as to call attention to specific financial concerns facing students. "There's this generalized anger that students are finally allowed to express," said walkout participant Jason Farbman, a graduate student at New York University. "Every student in school right now is looking at the prospect of zero employment, insane debts to go to school, and entering into a workforce with no jobs. These are kids from every walk of life who are doing exactly what they've been told to do in order to succeed and realizing that it's all a bunch of bull***t" (Fairbanks and Knafo 2011). Two weeks later, the student walkouts expanded to nearly 150 campuses. In addition, groups of students built encampments on school property at dozens of universities. In some cases, these actions by Occupy Colleges led to friction with administrators and confrontations with campus safety officers.

Many of the goals stated by Occupy Colleges protesters echoed those of the larger Occupy Wall Street movement, such as reducing income inequality, reining in corporate abuses, and giving ordinary citizens a voice in the political process. As members of the millennial generation preparing to enter the workforce, the student activists also expressed anger about what they viewed as short-sighted and irresponsible fiscal decision-making by earlier generations of leaders that left them to deal with massive budget deficits and a faltering social safety net. "They are wondering why society is making them pick up the check when they were not even invited to have dinner at the restaurant," John Pelletier explained in *Inside Higher Ed.* "They feel as though their future has been mortgaged for the benefit of the Wall Street elite and the baby boomers" (Pelletier 2011).

Occupy Colleges participants also expressed concern about the poor economic conditions awaiting them at graduation. As they prepared to enter the worst job market since the Great Depression, with record levels of unemployment for recent college graduates, many students felt angry and desperate. In the absence of other opportunities, some students found themselves working at minimum-wage jobs and living with their parents to save money. "If, say, you're a middle-aged investment banker, you might look around your social group and think the economy isn't doing all that bad," said Brayden King, a professor at Northwestern University. "But if you're a college student or a recent graduate, you're thinking the exact opposite when all of your friends are either unemployed or working in jobs that are much lower paying than what they expected to be doing after they graduated" (Fairbanks 2011).

The key issues for Occupy Colleges protesters also included rising tuition rates and student debt levels. They noted that college costs had increased at twice the rate of inflation since the 1980s while wages had remained relatively stagnant. As a result, young people increasingly depended on student loans to afford higher education and graduated with mountains of debt. Total outstanding student loan debt increased by 25 percent during the recession, the activists pointed out, and surpassed total credit card debt as a source of consumer obligation. "Student debt is a huge issue, with some students starting to question the wisdom of even having a degree anymore," said Joshua Christopher Harvey, a junior who organized protests at Texas State University. "There's only a six-month grace period to start paying our loans back—and we're worried there won't even be jobs available once we get out" (Fairbanks 2011).

Occupy Colleges marked the largest student movement since the 1970s, when the nation's college campuses erupted in protest against U.S. involvement in the Vietnam War. "Students' voices are demanding to be heard," said Conor Tomás Reed, a graduate student at the City University of New York. "It's a collective roar, and students are beyond disgusted and fed up. The time is especially ripe for this kind of mobilization" (Fairbanks and Knafo 2011). Although both the Occupy Colleges and Occupy Wall Street movements eventually faded out, some observers predicted that student participants would remain politically active and engaged members of society. "Our youth could channel their anger into a potent political force," Pelletier wrote. "The elites run the risk of underestimating the power of a large number of unemployed and underemployed educated young citizens armed with social media weapons to inflict significant damage" (Pelletier 2011).

Further Reading

Fairbanks, Amanda M. 2011. "Occupy Colleges: Student Supporters of Occupy Wall Street Continue to Show Solidarity." HuffPost, October 13, 2011. https://www.huffpost.com/entry/occupy-colleges-occupy-wall-street_n_1008619.

Fairbanks, Amanda M., and Saki Knafo. 2011. "College Sympathizers of Occupy Wall Street Walk Out of Class in Support." HuffPost, October 5, 2011. https://www.huffpost.com/entry/college-students-walk-out_n_996904.

Keller, Josh. 2011. "Public Colleges Struggle to Respond to Occupy Protests." *Chronicle of Higher Education*, November 16, 2011. https://www.chronicle.com/article/Public-Colleges-Struggle-to/129794.

Memoli, Michael A. 2011. "Obama: Occupy Wall Street Protests Show Americans' Frustration." *Los Angeles Times*, October 6, 2011. http://www.latimes.com/news/politics/la-pn-obama-occupy-wall-street-20111006,0,1992639.story.

Pelletier, John. 2011. "Why Occupy Colleges?" *Inside Higher Ed*, October 7, 2011. https://www.insidehighered.com/views/2011/10/07/why-occupy-colleges.

Reinicke, Carmen. 2018. "U.S. Income Inequality Continues to Grow." CNBC, July 19, 2018. https://www.cnbc.com/2018/07/19/income-inequality-continues-to-grow-in-the-united-states.html.

The "Operation Varsity Blues" College Admissions Scandal (2019)

In March 2019, dozens of prominent corporate executives and Hollywood celebrities became embroiled in "the largest college admissions scam ever prosecuted by the Department of Justice" (Huddleston 2019).

Code-named "Operation Varsity Blues," the case involved wealthy parents who paid a "consultant" a total of $25 million between 2011 and 2018 to falsify application details, inflate standardized test scores, embellish athletic accomplishments, or bribe college officials to ensure their children's admission to elite universities. When the cheating scandal came to light, it raised questions about the fairness of the admissions process at highly selective institutions, the role of college ratings in determining academic reputations and acceptance rates, and the wide disparities in educational access for students from different socioeconomic backgrounds.

Buying Admission to Elite Colleges

The Operation Varsity Blues college admissions investigation grew out of a separate Federal Bureau of Investigation (FBI) case against Los Angeles businessman Morrie Tobin for securities fraud. As part of a deal in exchange for lenient sentencing, Tobin provided federal authorities with information about a criminal conspiracy to rig the admissions process at prestigious universities in favor of specific students. Tobin acknowledged paying $450,000 to bribe the women's soccer coach at Yale University to designate his daughter as an athletic recruit in order to secure her admission to the Ivy League school, which typically accepted 6 out of every 100 applicants. Tobin's information led authorities to William "Rick" Singer, a college admissions consultant who ran two companies, The Key Worldwide Foundation and The Edge College and Career Network, that purported to improve students' chances of getting into the top schools.

Many affluent families hire legitimate consultants to give their children an edge in the competitive college admissions process. The independent educational consulting industry experienced rapid growth—quadrupling in size from 2005 to 2018—and took in an estimated $2 billion in 2019 (Newberry and Fry 2019). Legitimate consultants typically develop connections and insights by visiting the admissions offices of hundreds of colleges. They offer clients a wide range of services, from help selecting high-school courses and extracurricular activities, to advice for maximizing grade point averages and standardized test scores, to assistance with preparing college applications and writing essays. Consulting fees generally range from $2,000 to more than $10,000. "Money allows you to really engage with a different network of resources," said Wil Del Pilar of the nonprofit Education Trust, which works to increase educational opportunities for students from marginalized groups (Newberry and Fry 2019).

Singer, who pleaded guilty and cooperated with the FBI, went beyond the services offered by legitimate educational consultants and conspired to commit fraud on behalf of his clients. One of his schemes involved bribing college coaches to designate the children of wealthy clients as athletic recruits in tennis, soccer, rowing, water polo, volleyball, sailing, or other sports. Being listed as a recruited athlete greatly increased the students' chances for admission to elite colleges, even if they did not meet the usual academic criteria for the school in question. Actress Lori Loughlin and her husband, fashion designer Mossimo Giannulli, allegedly paid Singer $500,000 to arrange for their two daughters to be falsely identified as candidates for the crew team in order to secure their admission to the University of Southern California. Since the girls had never competed in crew, Singer created fake athletic profiles using photos of them sitting on rowing machines. Other Singer clients allegedly submitted forged credentials and fabricated photos with their child's head on another person's body to demonstrate their athletic accomplishments. "They would doctor up these fake resumes of all these athletic accolades," journalist Caroline Connolly explained. "And, as soon as the kid got in, they would come up with something like an injury, or whatever, so they would never actually play the sport. But they were on the roster and they got in as an athletic recruit" (Huddleston 2019).

Singer also facilitated cheating to help his clients' children improve their scores on college entrance exams, such as the Scholastic Aptitude Test (SAT). His methods included bribing psychologists to falsely claim that certain students had documented learning disabilities and thus required additional time or an environment free of distractions to take the SAT. Singer then arranged for those students to use "controlled" test locations with proctors that he selected. In some cases, Singer bribed exam administrators to correct wrong answers before submitting the test for scoring. In a few cases, Singer reportedly paid Mark Riddell—a Harvard University graduate who worked as an SAT tutor at an elite prep school—$10,000 to take the test in place of a client's child. "If your daughter took the SAT on her own the first time and got a particular score, retaking the exam, if her score goes up too much, that would invite scrutiny," federal prosecutor Andrew Lelling explained. "So Singer would discuss with parents what kind of score was impressive, but not too impressive, and then would instruct Riddell to attempt to get that score. And he was just good enough to do it" (Storey 2019).

Actress Felicity Huffman admitted paying Singer $15,000 to boost her older daughter's SAT score by more than 400 points, to 1420 out of 1600, and improve her ranking from the 35th to the 96th percentile nationally. Huffman pleaded guilty and received a sentence of 14 days in prison, a $30,000 fine, 250 hours of community service, and one year of probation. In announcing the sentence, Judge Indira Talwani told the Academy Award nominee, "The outrage is that in a system that is already so distorted by money and privilege ... you took the step of obtaining one more advantage to put your child ahead." Huffman apologized to hardworking students and parents who played by the rules. "In my desperation to be a good mother I talked myself into believing that all I was doing was giving my daughter a fair shot," she said. "I see the irony in that statement now because what I have done is the opposite of fair" (Klein et al. 2019).

Huffman was the first person to appear in court of the more than 50 people charged in the Operation Varsity Blues conspiracy. Singer faced up to 65 years in prison and a $1.25 million fine as the organizer of the scheme, which included charges related to misusing his nonprofit Key Foundation —which supposedly existed to help underprivileged students afford college—to launder payments from his wealthy clients. Federal prosecutors also announced charges against 33 parents of college applicants, 11 college coaches or athletic department officials, and several other university administrators and Singer associates. The indictments affected 8 prestigious academic institutions: Georgetown University, Stanford University, the University of California-Berkeley, the University of California-Los Angeles, the University of Southern California, the University of Texas-Austin, Wake Forest University, and Yale University.

Many of the students whose parents were implicated in the scandal did not know that their college admission came through fraudulent means. Some schools disciplined or expelled the students involved. In other cases, the students left school on their own accord after encountering hostility from fellow students on campus or on social media. Jack Buckingham, the son of a California businesswoman who paid to alter his SAT scores without his knowledge, apologized for his mother's actions. "I am upset that I was unknowingly involved in a large scheme that helps give kids who may not work as hard as others an advantage over those who truly deserve those spots. For that I am sorry," he stated. "I take comfort in the fact that this might help finally cut down on money and wealth being such a heavy factor in college admissions. Instead, I hope colleges may prioritize an applicant's character, intellect, and other qualities over everything else" (Yan 2019).

Raising Doubts about the Admissions Process

The admissions scandal made headlines across the country and generated public outrage. Many observers decried the role that wealth, privilege, and connections apparently played in college admissions. Critics charged that the actions of Singer and his clients harmed many hardworking, less fortunate students by denying them spots at elite colleges that they deserved. For instance, *The New Yorker* profiled Adam Langevin, a student who had been the top tennis player at Sage Hill School in California for four years as well as the 135th-ranked player nationally in his age group. Langevin watched in shock as one of his less-talented teammates, Grant Janavs, received an athletic scholarship to play NCAA Division I tennis at Georgetown University. "Grant is a nice person, but he's a god-awful tennis player," Langevin said. "I knew he wouldn't see a day on court. He would never play a match for Georgetown" (Golden and Burke 2019). Langevin eventually learned that the billionaire Janavs family had paid Singer $400,000 to bribe the Georgetown tennis coach to designate Grant as a recruited athlete, thus ensuring his acceptance to the prestigious school.

On a broader scale, the investigation raised questions about fairness and transparency in the college admissions process. It caused many potential college applicants and their families to worry about corruption in admissions, question the reputations of certain colleges and universities, or distrust the entire higher education system. In the wake of the scandal, the American Council of Education (ACE) convened focus groups across the United States to inquire about public attitudes toward higher education. Many people felt that they stood no chance of getting into an elite college without wealth and connections. "We kept hearing ... college isn't for us," said ACE president Ted Mitchell. "We heard that [admissions] is a game they couldn't play, it wasn't real, they were at a disadvantage" (Willen 2020). Confirming these views, researchers found that children from families in the top 1 percent income bracket were 77 times more likely to attend a top-ranked, private college than children from families in the lowest 20 percent of earners (Newberry and Fry 2019). In fact, less than 1 out of every 200 children from the poorest fifth of American households attended an elite university. "Looking at students based on income buckets, selective institutions and inequality go hand in hand," said Nick Hillman, a professor of education at the University of Wisconsin (Willen 2020).

The scandal also reignited longstanding debates over affirmative action in higher education. Opponents of these programs traditionally argued that they gave unfair advantages to students from minority groups and penalized more deserving students from majority groups. They asserted that the goal of student-body diversity did not justify using racial and ethnic preferences in college admissions. Supporters of affirmative action viewed the scandal as proof that the U.S. higher education system was biased in favor of wealthy white students. "There's a lot more kids at elite colleges because their parents are rich than because they're brown or black," noted one proponent (Blake 2019). They argued that minority students had no opportunity to get ahead without affirmative action programs to level the playing field in college admissions.

Critics pointed out that children from wealthy families enjoyed many advantages not available to their less fortunate peers, even without resorting to cheating and bribery. Throughout their years of primary and secondary education, for instance, affluent students were more likely to have access to fancy prep schools, knowledgeable guidance counselors, advanced coursework, private tutors, and SAT preparation courses. They were also more likely to have opportunities to take music lessons and participate in expensive "country club" sports to improve their chances of earning college scholarships. Students from wealthy families also had the resources to travel across the country and visit college campuses prior to submitting applications. A 2017 survey conducted by the National Association for College Admission Counseling found that 40 percent of schools considered campus visits—known as "demonstrated interest" by prospective students—as a factor in undergraduate admissions decisions (Newberry and Fry 2019).

The admissions process at many elite colleges and universities—including Cornell, Harvard, and USC—also granted preferential treatment to the children of alumni. Research suggested that these "legacy" admissions accounted for up to 25 percent of the student body at some schools (Newberry and Fry 2019). In addition, some extremely wealthy parents influenced admissions decisions in favor of their children by making legal, tax-deductible monetary donations to top institutions. In his book *The Price of Admission: How America's Ruling Class Buys Its Way into Elite Colleges—And Who Gets Left Outside the Gates,* Daniel Golden noted that Jared Kushner —son-in-law and senior adviser to President Donald Trump—received admission to Harvard after his father donated $2.5 million to the university in 1998. Although Kushner denied receiving special treatment, his acceptance shocked administrators at his New Jersey prep school. "His GPA did not warrant it, his SAT scores did not warrant it. We thought, for sure, there was no way this was going to happen," one official told Golden. "Then, lo and behold, Jared was accepted. It was a little bit disappointing because there were at the time other kids we thought should really get in on the merits, and they did not" (Golden 2016).

The built-in advantages enjoyed by students from wealthy families also helps them earn merit scholarships—a form of institutional financial aid or "tuition discounting" awarded in college admissions to attract highly qualified applicants and convince them to enroll. "If you pick any two freshmen at the same college, they are likely to be paying completely different tuition rates," Paul Tough wrote in *The Years That Matter Most: How College Makes or Breaks Us.* "Those rates are based not on the true value of the service the college is offering or even on the ability of the students' family to pay; instead, they are based on a complex calculation of what the student is worth to the college and what the college is worth to the student" (Tough 2019, 163). The student performance criteria used in awarding merit-based aid—such as grade point average, class rank, and SAT scores—tends to correlate with family income. As a result, affluent students often receive more financial assistance than less privileged students, even though they have less financial need. The predominantly affluent students who attend private colleges receive an average of $25,000 per year in merit aid, for example, while the lower-income students who attend public community colleges receive an average of $8,000 per year. "In other words, our system gives three times as much aid to the least needy as it gives to the most," Adam Davidson commented in the *New York Times Magazine* (Davidson 2015).

Experts suggested many ways to change the college admissions process to make it more transparent and to help restore public trust in higher education. Some recommended discontinuing practices that gave preferential treatment to legacies, donors, and athletes. Others called on elite schools to reserve more spots for low-income and first-generation college students. Many critics of the college admissions process suggested overhauling the college ranking systems employed by *U.S. News and World Report* and other sources, claiming that they put pressure on schools to admit only the highest-achieving students and to reject large numbers of applicants in order to maintain a reputation for selectivity. In a poll of National Association of College Admissions Counselors (NACAC) members, 87 percent acknowledged making decisions counterproductive to their institution's educational mission in an effort to improve its ranking (Tough 2019, 159).

Although college rankings helped families compare educational options and make informed choices, critics claimed that they also created intense competition for students to gain admission to the "best" schools—and thus fostered an environment ripe for the type of cheating that characterized the Operation Varsity Blues scandal. Instead, critics suggested creating a rankings system that rewarded schools for promoting affordability and access and taking positive steps to eliminate the stratification of higher education. "We talk a lot about merit in this country. We want kids to get in based on the work that they've put in," said Wil Del Pilar of the nonprofit Education Trust. "What we don't acknowledge is that not everyone begins from the same starting line" (Newberry and Fry 2019).

Further Reading

Blake, John. 2019. "The College Admissions Scam Opens a New Front in the Affirmative Action Debate." CNN, March 17, 2019. https://www.cnn.com/2019/03/17/us/college-cheating-scandal-affirmative-action-debate/index.html.

Davidson, Adam. 2015. "Is College Tuition Really Too High?" *New York Times Magazine,* September 13, 2015. https://www.nytimes.com/2015/09/13/magazine/is-college-tuition-too-high.html?_r=1.

Golden, Daniel. 2006. *The Price of Admission: How America's Ruling Class Buys Its Way into Elite Colleges—And Who Gets Left Outside the Gates.* New York: Random House.

Golden, Daniel. 2016. "How Did 'Less Than Stellar' High School Student Jared Kushner Get into Harvard?" *Guardian,* November 18, 2016. https://www.theguardian.com/commentisfree/2016/nov/18/jared-kushner-harvard-donald-trump-son-in-law.

Golden, Daniel, and Doris Burke. 2019. "The Unseen Student Victims of the 'Varsity Blues' College Admissions Scandal." *The New Yorker,* October 8, 2019. https://www.newyorker.com/books/page-turner/the-unseen-student-victims-of-the-varsity-blues-college-admissions-scandal.

Huddleston, Tom, Jr. 2019. "How an Ex-Basketball Coach Tried to Pull Off the Biggest College Admissions Scam Ever, Allegedly Roping in CEOs and Celebs." CNBC, August 11, 2019. https://www.cnbc.com/2019/08/11/american-greed-inside-college-admissions-scandal.html.

Kirkland, Justin. 2019. "The Lori Loughlin and Felicity Huffman College Admissions Scam Is So Much Bigger Than Two Celebrities." *Esquire,* March 12, 2019. https://www.esquire.com/entertainment/a26800556/operation-varsity-blues-explainer/.

Klein, Asher, Alysha Palumbo, Monica Madeja, and Karla Rendon-Alvarez. 2019. "Felicity Huffman Sentenced to Prison Time in College Cheating Scandal." NBC 10 Boston, September 13, 2019. https://www.nbcboston.com/news/local/felicity-huffman-college-admission-cheating-scheme-sentencing/1837945/.

Newberry, Laura, and Hannah Fry. 2019. "The Legal Way the Rich Get Their Kids into Elite Colleges: Huge Donations for Years." *Los Angeles Times,* March 22, 2019. https://www.latimes.com/local/lanow/la-me-ln-college-admissions-scandal-legal-ways-20190318-story.html.

Storey, Kate. 2019. "Mark Riddell Allegedly Made $10,000 for Each SAT Test He Took in College Admissions Scam." *Esquire,* March 13, 2019. https://www.esquire.com/news-politics/a26809066/mark-riddell-college-admissions-scam-exam-taker/.

Strauss, Valerie. 2020. "There's a Lot of Talk about Changing College Admissions after the Varsity Blues Scandal—Don't Hold Your Breath." *Washington Post,* February 15, 2020. https://www.washingtonpost.com/education/2020/02/15/theres-lot-talk-about-changing-college-admissions-after-varsity-blues-scandal-dont-hold-your-breath/.

Tough, Paul. 2019. *The Years That Matter Most: How College Makes or Breaks Us.* Boston: Houghton Mifflin.

Willen, Liz. 2020. "After 'Varsity Blues' Scandal, Lots of Talk about Overhauling College Admissions. Will There Be Action?" *Hechinger Report,* February 4,

2020. https://hechingerreport.org/after-varsity-blues-scandal-lots-of-talk-about-overhauling-college-admissions-will-there-be-action/.

Yan, Holly. 2019. "What We Know So Far in the College Admissions Cheating Scandal." CNN, March 19, 2019. https://www.cnn.com/2019/03/13/us/what-we-know-college-admissions-cheating-scandal/index.html.

CHAPTER THREE

Impacts of the College Affordability Crisis

This chapter examines the impact of the college affordability and student debt crises on the people affected by them and on American society. It reviews evidence showing that income-based disparities in college access reinforce economic inequality in the United States. It explores how the rising costs of college contribute to food insecurity and homelessness among low-income students. Next, the chapter charts the impact of student loan debt on the U.S. economy and on the lives of individual borrowers. It also analyzes proposals for tuition-free college and student-loan forgiveness advanced by 2020 Democratic presidential candidates and other policymakers.

College Affordability and Income Inequality

During the early twenty-first century, income inequality in the United States reached levels not seen since the Gilded Age a hundred years earlier. Whereas the top 10 percent of earners accounted for around one-third of the nation's total income in the 1970s, this share grew to nearly 50 percent by the 2010s (Hill 2013). Throughout history, many Americans viewed higher education as a pathway to social mobility and economic prosperity. Earning a college degree enabled people to get good jobs, increase their income, raise their families out of poverty, and contribute to society. To achieve these outcomes and gain the competitive benefits of an educated workforce, the U.S. government actively promoted access to higher education for low-income citizens. The Higher Education Act of 1965 and its reauthorizations, for instance, established a system of need-based financial aid to help make college more affordable for high-achieving students of limited means.

Despite such efforts, however, critics charge that the American system of higher education has increasingly favored students from wealthy backgrounds. Research shows that affluent students are more likely to enroll in college, qualify for merit-based financial aid, attend elite private colleges and flagship public universities, complete degree programs, and embark on lucrative professional careers than their less fortunate peers of similar academic ability. Rather than serving as a socioeconomic equalizer, according to critics, the U.S. higher education system exacerbates income inequality and reinforces class distinctions. Earning a college degree "was once the gleaming star and the centerpiece of the American dream, because it was the mechanism through which you could achieve anything," said sociologist Laura Hamilton. "But the golden period of higher education, when the government really partnered with schools to really create educational opportunities for people regardless of their backgrounds, that moment is gone. It's thoroughly gone" (Marcus and Hacker 2015).

Income-Based Disparities in Higher Education

The economic disparities in higher education begin with college enrollment. Whereas 80 percent of children from families in the top income quartile typically attend college, only 30 percent of children from families in the bottom income quartile do so (Goldrick-Rab et al. 2016). This stark difference is unrelated to academic ability. Even among high-achieving students from low-income families—those who receive top scores on eighth-grade standardized tests—only 50 percent continue on to college (Marcus and Hacker 2015). "If you're a bright kid coming from a relatively low-income family, your chances of enrolling in and eventually completing college are much, much lower than a less-talented student coming from a wealthy family," said Cornell University economist Ron Ehrenberg (Marcus 2017).

Researchers offer a number of explanations for income-based differences in college enrollment. The expense associated with higher education undoubtedly creates a major barrier for many students from low-income families. Yet these students often face obstacles before they even apply to college, such as underperforming schools that fail to provide preparatory coursework, overwhelmed high-school counselors who fail to offer information and guidance, and inadequate resources to help them prepare for college-admissions tests, fill out college applications, and apply for financial aid.

Such factors pose particular challenges for first-generation college students, who often must navigate the complexities of the college admissions process without parental assistance. "If you come from a community where your parents went to college, and it's part of the dinnertime conversation, then it's in your expectations," said Doris Arrington, dean of student services at a community college. "Many of our students don't have that kind of information" (Marcus and Hacker 2015). In contrast, many students from wealthy families attend high-performing schools and have greater access to advanced coursework, tutors, counselors, test-preparation services, and college admissions consultants. Affluent students also have more opportunities to enhance their college applications through participation in extracurricular activities and community service.

These factors contribute to vast disparities in the types of colleges attended by students from different socioeconomic backgrounds. Research shows that children from families in the top 1 percent income bracket are 77 times more likely to attend a top-ranked, private college than children from families in the lowest 20 percent of earners (Whistle and Hiler 2019). As a result, more of the students enrolled at highly selective U.S. colleges and universities come from the top 1 percent than from the bottom 60 percent, and students from the lowest quartile account for only 3 percent of enrollment at these prestigious institutions (Taylor 2018). One critic described the preponderance of wealthy students at elite schools as "polishing the privileged" (Marcus 2017). "Differences in enrollment patterns by family income reflect the stratification of the financial, academic, and other resources that are required to enroll in different colleges and universities," wrote researchers Laura Perna and Roman Ruiz. "Students from higher-income families have the resources that enable meaningful choice from among the array of available options nationwide. But resource constraints and structural failures often limit the 'choices' of students from lower-income families" (Zinshteyn 2016).

According to the College Board, 6.8 million undergraduate students—or about 31 percent—received federal Pell Grants in 2018-2019, meaning that they demonstrated exceptional financial need (most recipients reported family income of around $30,000 or less) (College Board 2020). Yet most elite schools enrolled a much smaller percentage of low-income students. At such prestigious private universities as Brown, Columbia, Duke, Georgetown, Stanford, and Yale, Pell Grant recipients comprised an average of 15 percent of undergraduate students. Such taxpayer-funded flagship public institutions as the universities of Colorado, Michigan, Pennsylvania, Virginia, and Wisconsin demonstrated a similar lack of economic diversity, with Pell Grant recipients making up less than 20 percent of undergraduate enrollment. A study conducted by Georgetown University researchers found that at least 86,000 more low-income students per year possessed the academic qualifications required for admission to highly selective institutions than received the opportunity to enroll (Marcus 2017). "The gap between the haves and the have-nots is just getting bigger," said Perna.

"Really it calls into question the American dream. We tell people, just work hard and you'll have these opportunities available. The reality is, if you grow up in a [low-income] neighborhood…, your chances are quite different than if you grow up just a few miles away in a family with a quite higher income" (Marcus and Hacker 2015).

Rather than attending selective institutions with strong academic reputations and high graduation rates, many low-income students go to local community colleges, nonselective regional public universities, or open-enrollment for-profit colleges. A Pew Research study found that the average share of undergraduate students in poverty ranged from 13 percent at highly selective four-year institutions, to 25 percent at minimally selective four-year institutions, to 27 percent at two-year public community colleges, to 36 percent at private, for-profit colleges (Fry and Cilluffo 2019). Although community colleges offer students a low-cost option, many have struggled since the 2008 recession with steep reductions in state funding, which affects the quality of facilities, amenities, services, and instruction they offer. On average, community colleges spend around half as much per student on instruction than public four-year universities and around one-third as much per student as private nonprofit colleges (National Center for Education Statistics 2019). While 81 percent of community college students express a desire to transfer to a four-year institution, however, only 12 percent manage to do so. "The low-income students really want to be somewhere else," said Maureen Hoyler of the Council for Opportunity in Education. "If they had a choice,… they would want the same opportunity of the students at the private colleges" (Marcus and Hacker 2015).

In addition, low-income students eligible for federal Pell Grants are three times more likely than wealthier students to enroll in private, for-profit colleges such as ITT Technical Institute, DeVry University, and the University of Phoenix (Zinshteyn 2016). Although these schools tend to charge high tuition rates, they lure vulnerable students with promises of proprietary educational programs that supposedly offer access to high-paying careers. Instead, many for-profit schools provide substandard instruction and generate poor educational outcomes, including low graduation rates and high levels of student loan debt. Several for-profit colleges were forced to close after coming under federal scrutiny for deceiving and defrauding students. "We don't need a dual system of higher education where rich people get one thing and poor people get another thing," Hoyler stated, "especially if what they get is kind of a lie" (Marcus and Hacker 2015).

The income-based disparities in higher education also extend to rates of degree completion. Among Pell Grant recipients who enroll at public universities, 11 percent drop out of college after one year, and 80 percent fail to complete a bachelor's degree within four years (Goldrick-Rab et al. 2016). Another study found that 60 percent of students from the top quartile income bracket earned bachelor's degrees within ten years of graduating from high school, compared to only 15 percent of students from the lowest quartile (Zinshteyn 2016). Research also suggests that the disparity in college completion rates between high- and low-income students is growing. Whereas 24-year-olds from the upper half of the income distribution accounted for 72 percent of bachelor's degrees awarded in 1970, the percentage increased to 77 percent by 2014 (Zinshteyn 2016). "Their chances of really graduating from college are very low," Hoyler said of low-income students. "And the burden's all on them—you know, take out loans and then don't graduate" (Marcus and Hacker 2015).

Sociologists note many factors that make it more difficult for students from low-income families to remain in college and earn degrees. Many students must work at part-time jobs while enrolled in college to earn money for tuition and living expenses. Hours spent working leave students with less time to attend classes, study, and sleep, which can inhibit their academic performance. For low-income students who attend elite institutions, the need to work may also increase awareness of class distinctions and feelings of marginalization, which may influence their decision to leave school before completing a degree. "You can think of it as a luxury cruise," Hamilton explained. "There are the people who are there to enjoy their four-year vacation, and people who are there to serve them. The only interaction that poor students have with wealthy students is picking up their towels at the [campus] gym or washing their dishes in the cafeteria" (Marcus and Hacker 2015). Low-income students attending community colleges or nonselective public universities, on the other hand, often end up dropping out because they lack access to academic counseling and support services to help them stay on track with course selection and degree requirements. "There are just fewer ways to fail at more prestigious schools," Hamilton noted. "But when you go down the ladder, there's a lot less of that kind of support" (Marcus and Hacker 2015).

Financial Aid and Affordability

For most low-income students, however, cost is the determining factor in whether they complete a college degree. While most low-income students qualify for need-based financial aid, studies show that the amounts provided have not kept up with the rapid growth in college costs. During the 2019-2020 academic year, for instance, the maximum federal Pell Grant amount of $6,095 only covered 28 percent of the average published tuition, fees, and room and board costs at public four-year universities. For Pell Grant recipients who enrolled at private, nonprofit colleges, the amount only covered 12 percent of the average published costs (College Board 2020). In the early 1970s, by comparison, the maximum Pell Grant covered nearly 75 percent of the average cost of college (Goldrick-Rab et al. 2016).

Researchers have also noted a shift in financial aid away from need-based grants that benefit low-income students and toward tax breaks and merit-based scholarships that mainly benefit wealthier students. The federal work-study program, which enables students to earn money for college by working at subsidized campus jobs, provides a significant portion of its $1 billion annual funding to students without financial need. The federal formula used to allocate work-study funds gives 38 percent to private colleges, which enroll predominantly high-income students, and only 20 percent to community colleges, which enroll predominantly low-income students (Marcus 2017). As a result, one study found that nearly 20 percent of work-study recipients came from families with annual incomes over $100,000 (Marcus and Hacker 2015).

Several other federal programs aimed at increasing access to higher education benefit affluent families almost exclusively. Under Section 529 of the Internal Revenue Code, families are allowed to establish tax-advantaged savings accounts to pay college expenses for a designated beneficiary. Contributions to 529 plans are tax deductible at the state level, while distributions are exempt from federal tax when used for qualified education expenses. Critics charge that nearly all of the tax benefits go to wealthy families who would send their children to college without them. Only 3 percent of Americans take advantage of the opportunity to invest in a college-savings account, and those who do have household wealth 25 times higher than the median (Hsu 2019). In fact, one survey found that only 20 percent of families with annual incomes under $35,000 were even aware of 529 plans (Marcus 2017).

The federal government also offers income tax deductions for tuition paid to accredited institutions of higher learning. The American Opportunity Tax Credit costs the federal government $35 billion per year in foregone revenue, which exceeds the $28 billion in annual federal expenditures for Pell Grants. Yet the Congressional Research Service reported that more than one-fifth of the tax credits went to families earning between $100,000 and $180,000 per year (Marcus 2017). "Lots of higher education policies are built in a way that would win support from middle- and even upper-income taxpayers and they were not really thought about as, 'Will this really increase the number of people going to college?'" Ehrenberg explained. "If I were a social planner, we would be using our resources to help support the people who would not be able to go to college" (Marcus 2017).

Many colleges and universities offer financial aid to prospective students, but a growing share of institutional aid takes the form of merit-based scholarships for students' academic, athletic, or artistic performance. According to the U.S. Department of Education, the percentage of aid awarded for reasons other than financial need doubled between 1995 and 2015 (Marcus and Hacker 2015). The criteria used in awarding merit-based aid—such as grade point average, class rank, SAT scores, and extracurricular activities—tend to correlate with family income. As a result, affluent students often receive more financial assistance than less privileged students, even though they have less financial need. The predominantly affluent students who attend private colleges receive an average of $25,000 per year in merit aid, for example, while the lower-income students who attend public community colleges receive an average of $8,000 per year. "In other words, our system gives three times as much aid to the least needy as it gives to the most," Adam Davidson commented in the *New York Times Magazine* (Davidson 2015).

According to the Education Trust, both public and private four-year institutions awarded more than half of their total financial aid to their most affluent students in 2017 (Taylor 2018). In many cases, admissions officers use merit-based aid to attract highly qualified students whose scores and statistics will raise the school's national ranking. "We've almost built this system that isn't set up to open its doors to low-income students," said Angel Pérez, vice president of enrollment at Trinity College in Connecticut. "Take too many and your average GPA or SAT scores decrease. There goes your *U.S. News* ranking. Admit students who don't have the best stats and you might damage your yield and retention numbers. There goes your Moody's bond rating" (Marcus and Hacker 2015).

As schools channeled more financial aid funds toward middle- and upper-income students, undergraduates in the lowest income quartile faced an average of $9,100 per year in unmet financial need—defined as the cost of attendance remaining after deducting expected family contribution, grants, scholarships, and other discounts (excluding loans). Students in the top two income quartiles, on the other hand, received financial aid in excess of what the federal formula indicated that their families should expect to contribute toward college costs (Pell Institute 2019). Critics asserted that the shift away from need-based aid limited the educational opportunities available to low-income students while forcing them to take on debt to afford college. "There is a very seriously warped view among many Americans, and particularly more affluent Americans, about where the money is actually going," said Brookings Institution economist Richard Reeves. "They say, look, there's always other support going to poorer kids.... Well, there isn't. There actually isn't. But the ignorance about where the money is actually going and who benefits from it, that ignorance is really an obstacle to reform around what is in fact a reverse distribution" (Marcus 2017).

Critics assert that income-based disparities in educational attainment exacerbate the problem of economic inequality in the United States. "College-going, once associated with opportunity, now engenders the creation of something that increasingly resembles a caste system," Suzanne Mettler wrote in *Degrees of Inequality*. "It takes Americans who grew up in different social strata and it widens the divisions between them and makes them more rigid. The consequences are vast, ranging from differences in employment rates and lifetime earnings to health and civic engagement" (Mettler 2014, 5). Studies have shown that recipients of bachelor's degrees earn around twice as much throughout their careers as people with only high-school diplomas. In addition, one report predicted that two-thirds of all new jobs created in 2020 and beyond would require a college education (Zinshteyn 2016). An educated workforce also conveys economic benefits to society in the form of increases in productivity, innovation, job creation, and tax revenues, as well as decreases in health care costs, incarceration rates, and reliance on public assistance. "Once students drop out of community college, taxpayers will continue to pay their bills," Davidson explained. "That's not called education funding; it's called welfare or criminal-justice or health care expenditures.... In an economy that demands and rewards education, those who have it will pay the bills for those who don't" (Davidson 2015).

Policymakers and institutions of higher learning are seeking ways to eliminate socioeconomic barriers and improve college attainment for students from low-income backgrounds. Many proposals center around increasing the percentage of state and federal financial aid awarded on the basis of need. Some advocates suggest increasing the maximum Pell Grant to around $15,000 per year and requiring states to provide partial funding. Increasing education grants could help low-income students remain in college and avoid student loan debt by covering the cost of books, living expenses, and other out-of-pocket costs in addition to tuition. These students could also work fewer hours, giving them more time to study and increasing their ability to maintain satisfactory progress toward degrees. Other proposals involve expanding access to technical training and vocational education to provide nonacademic career paths for students who cannot afford or do not wish to attend college. Critics of these proposals contend that pushing low-income students into nonacademic "tracks" unfairly limits their educational opportunities.

Some critics argue that colleges and universities, rather than government, should take responsibility for increasing the economic diversity of their student bodies and raising completion rates for low-income students. They point out that the nation's most prestigious private colleges have billions of dollars in endowments and typically post annual budget surpluses, giving them ample funding to increase need-based financial aid. Instead, these schools often compete to admit wealthy students who can afford to pay the full price of attendance by offering state-of-the-art facilities, gourmet meal options, and other expensive amenities and services. Such competition creates a cycle of increased spending, rising tuition rates, and shifts toward merit-based aid, with few schools willing to buck the trend. In this way, widening economic inequality fuels the college affordability crisis, just as the barriers to college access for low-income students perpetuate income inequality.

Further Reading

College Board. 2020. "Pell Grants: Recipients, Maximum Pell, and Average Pell." https://research.collegeboard.org/trends/student-aid/figures-tables/pell-grants-recipients-maximum-pell-and-average-pell.

Davidson, Adam. 2015. "Is College Tuition Really Too High?" *New York Times Magazine,* September 13, 2015. https://www.nytimes.com/2015/09/13/magazine/is-college-tuition-too-high.html?_r=1.

Deruy, Emily. 2017. "Measuring College (Un)Affordability." *Atlantic,* March 23, 2017. https://www.theatlantic.com/education/archive/2017/03/measuring-college-unaffordability/520476/.

Fry, Richard, and Anthony Cilluffo. 2019. "A Rising Share of Undergraduate Students Are from Poor Families, Especially at Less Selective Colleges." Pew Research Center, May 22, 2019. https://www.pewsocialtrends.org/2019/05/22/a-rising-share-of-undergraduates-are-from-poor-families-especially-at-less-selective-colleges/.

Goldrick-Rab, Sara, Robert Kelchen, Douglas N. Harris, and James Benson. 2016. "Reducing Income Inequality in Educational Attainment: Experimental Evidence on the Impact of Financial Aid on College Completion." *American Journal of Sociology* 121(6): 1762–1817. https://hope4college.com/wp-content/uploads/2018/09/Goldrick-Rab-etal-Reducing-Income-Inequality-in-Educational-Attainment.pdf.

Hill, Catherine B. 2013. "Higher Education's Biggest Challenge Is Income Inequality." *Washington Post,* September 6, 2013. https://www.washingtonpost.com/opinions/higher-educations-biggest-challenge-is-income-inequality/2013/09/06/94b809a8-15ac-11e3-be6e-dc6ae8a5b3a8_story.html.

Hsu, Hua. 2019. "Student Debt Is Transforming the American Family." *New Yorker,* September 2, 2019. https://www.newyorker.com/magazine/2019/09/09/student-debt-is-transforming-the-american-family.

Marcus, Jon. 2017. "In an Era of Inequity, More and More College Financial Aid Is Going to the Rich." Hechinger Report, December 7, 2017. https://hechingerreport.org/era-inequity-college-financial-aid-going-rich/.

Marcus, Jon, and Holly K. Hacker. 2015. "The Rich-Poor Divide on America's College Campuses Is Getting Wider, Fast." Hechinger Report, December 17, 2015. https://hechingerreport.org/the-socioeconomic-divide-on-americas-college-campuses-is-getting-wider-fast/.

Mettler, Suzanne. 2014. *Degrees of Inequality: How the Politics of Higher Education Sabotaged the American Dream.* New York: Basic Books.

National Center for Education Statistics. 2019. "Postsecondary Institution Expenses." *The Condition of Education 2019* (NCES 2019-144). https://nces.ed.gov/fastfacts/display.asp?id=75.

Pell Institute. 2019. "Indicators of Higher Education Equity in the United States: 2019 Historical Trend Report." http://pellinstitute.org/downloads/publications-Indicators_of_Higher_Education_Equity_in_the_US_2019_Historical_Trend_Report.pdf.

Taylor, Kelley. 2018. "College Affordability Guides Provoke Debate, Action on Economic Inequality on Campus." *Insight into Diversity,* October 18, 2018. https://www.insightintodiversity.com/college-affordability-guides-provoke-debate-action-on-economic-inequality-on-campuses/.

Whistle, Wesley, and Tamara Hiler. 2019. "Why Free College Could Increase Inequality." Third Way, March 19, 2019. https://www.thirdway.org/memo/why-free-college-could-increase-inequality.

Zinshteyn, Mikhail. 2016. "The Growing College-Degree Wealth Gap." *Atlantic,* April 25, 2016. https://www.theatlantic.com/education/archive/2016/04/the-growing-wealth-gap-in-who-earns-college-degrees/479688/.

Hunger and Homelessness among College Students

Being broke, scrounging for spare change to buy food, and subsisting on cheap and easy meals of ramen noodles, cereal, or peanut-butter-and-jelly sandwiches were long considered the hallmarks of a stereotypical college student's existence. As the costs associated with higher education increased at more than twice the rate of inflation, however, surveys revealed that food insecurity—defined as limited or uncertain access to affordable, nutritious meals—was a real problem affecting an estimated 40 percent of students on college campuses across the United States. "The prevalence of food insecurity among college students is a symptom of the increasing unaffordability of higher education in America," according to the Center for American Progress. "Policymakers must grapple with students' living costs—including food and housing—in any effort to make college affordable. A system that allows college students to struggle with food insecurity as they try to focus on their studies shortchanges them of their opportunity to build a better life" (Barboy 2019).

Food Insecurity on Campus

The concept of food insecurity aroused some controversy as researchers debated how to define and measure it. The U.S. Department of Agriculture and other sources differentiated food insecurity from hunger, which referred to an individual's physical discomfort from consuming insufficient food to support an active, healthy lifestyle. Food insecurity, on the other hand, related to inadequate financial resources to provide an individual with consistent access to a varied, nutritious diet. Only individuals with very low food security typically experienced persistent hunger from limited food intake. People with low or marginal food security experienced anxiety about the quality or sufficiency of available food, along with the possibility of intermittent food shortages and occasional hunger.

The difficulty in defining and measuring food insecurity led to variation in estimates of its prevalence among college students. A 2018 survey of 86,000 students at 123 colleges and universities conducted by the Hope Center for College, Community, and Justice at Temple University found that 45 percent of respondents had experienced food insecurity in the previous 30 days. The numbers ranged from 41 percent of students at four-year universities to 48 percent of students at two-year community colleges (Hope Center 2020). A similar survey conducted by the Wisconsin HOPE Lab involved 43,000 students at 66 colleges and universities. It found that 36 percent of university students and 42 percent of community college students had experienced food insecurity in the previous month (Goldrick-Rab et al. 2018). The nonpartisan Government Accountability Office (GAO) reviewed the results of 31 other studies and estimated that at least 30 percent of college students nationwide experienced food insecurity (Harris 2019a). With nearly 20 million students enrolled in U.S. institutions of higher learning in 2019, these estimates meant that food insecurity affected between 6 million and 8 million students.

Most estimates showed a significantly higher prevalence of food insecurity among college students than the 11 to 12 percent generally found in the overall U.S. population. Some observers blamed the high costs of college for the fact that so many students struggled to afford food and meet other basic needs. "This population is particularly vulnerable to going hungry," Adam Harris wrote in *The Atlantic,* "as many are spending all available funds on costs associated with school, and holding down a full-time job—let alone a lucrative one—can be incredibly difficult" (Harris 2019b).

Although most low-income students qualified for state and federal grants and other financial aid to help pay tuition costs, these funds did not necessarily cover living expenses, which accounted for more than half the cost of attendance at some schools. According to the College Board (2019), a typical community college student had $400 in aid money left over after paying tuition and fees to put toward other expenses. Yet full-time students faced average room and board costs of more than $8,000 at two-year community colleges and nearly $11,000 at four-year public universities during the 2017-2018 academic year (Andrews 2018). While most colleges offered meal plans for students, the cost often exceeded the budgets of low-income students. Columbia University, for instance, charged first-year undergraduate students $2,800 per semester for a basic meal plan—or about as much as an average American spent on food for an entire year (Otero-Amad 2019).

The GAO report pointed out that only 29 percent of college students fit into the "traditional" category, meaning that they enrolled in college immediately after graduating from high school and continued to rely on their parents for financial support. The other 71 percent had one or more "nontraditional" factors, such as delayed college enrollment, part-time college attendance, full-time employment, financial independence, or dependent children. Researcher Katharine Broton at the University of Iowa found that 25 percent of college students had children of their own, while 40 percent worked at least part-time while going to school. "Most of the students, we find, are working *and* receiving financial aid, but still struggling with food insecurity," she said (Andrews 2018).

Nontraditional students, first-generation college students, and students from low-income backgrounds ranked among the most likely to struggle to afford college. Many students in these groups chose to attend two-year community colleges to save money. A Wisconsin HOPE Lab survey of 33,000 students at 70 community colleges found that two-thirds of respondents experienced food insecurity, while half also experienced housing insecurity, which was defined as lacking the funds to pay rent and utilities or being forced to move often. In addition, 14 percent of community college students reported being homeless. Among the students facing food and housing insecurity, one-third had jobs and received financial aid, while another third financed their education with student loans, yet these funds did not cover their living expenses (Bendix 2017).

Although food insecurity was most common among students from low-income backgrounds, researcher Sara Goldrick-Rab noted that it also affected some middle-class students, whom she described as "too rich for Pell [Grants] and too poor to afford college" (Harris 2019a).

Trellis Company, which offers programs and services to help at-risk students complete college and repay education loans, followed 72 students through an academic year. The researchers found that the students' vulnerability to food security fluctuated depending on their financial circumstances. The 26 participants whose food security declined over the course of the study encountered unexpected expenses, such as car repairs or health care costs, or experienced a loss of income due to business hardship, layoffs, or reduced hours. These students responded by reducing their food intake or consuming lower-quality meals to conserve funds. The 30 participants whose food security improved during the study either received additional income, such as a pay raise or financial help from family members, or saved money by adhering to a budget, cooking at home, taking in a roommate, or moving to cheaper housing (Barboy 2019).

Students affected by food insecurity experienced many negative effects on their lives and health that made it difficult for them to succeed in college. Financial anxiety and inadequate nutrition contributed to sleep loss, inability to concentrate, and vulnerability to illness. Some students responded to food insecurity by working long hours, which left them with limited free time to study or engage in stress-relieving social activities (Barboy 2019). Financial challenges and food insecurity also negatively affected students' academic performance, increasing the likelihood that they would receive poor grades, lose merit scholarships, drop out of college before completing a degree, and struggle to repay education loans. This situation, in turn, decreased the likelihood that they would obtain high-paying jobs and contribute to society. Some observers argued that food insecurity among college students thus caused financial aid funding to go to waste. "Food insecurity is a college-completion issue," Goldrick-Rab declared. "We're undermining our federal investment in financial aid by not paying attention to this. We have to stop pretending like living expenses are not educational expenses" (Harris 2019a).

Approaches to Help Struggling Students

Many colleges responded to reports of food insecurity among students by building food pantries on campus. As of 2019, more than 700 schools nationwide participated in the College and University Food Bank Alliance, with members including community colleges as well as Ivy League universities (Laterman 2019). In New York, Governor Andrew Cuomo required all public universities in the state to establish food pantries for students. The food pantry at the University of California-Berkeley—located in one of the most expensive areas of the United States—typically served around 1,000 students per week. It offered fresh produce from local farmers' markets and other nutritious foods free to anyone with a student ID. Reniel Del Rosario, a full-time student who also worked more than 20 hours per week at a work-study job, faced food insecurity due to the high costs of tuition, books, and rent. "I feel like I did have to go hungry," he acknowledged, and sometimes "had to limit myself to the amount of food for the week because I had to save money for other things." Del Rosario became a regular patron of the food pantry at Berkeley. "Going to a 99-cent store or the dollar store for groceries wasn't ideal," he recalled. "Being able to get fresh produce and things that are more nutritional helped me a lot" (Otero-Amad 2019).

A group of students at the University of California-Los Angeles founded the Swipe Out Hunger program to allow students to donate unused meal plan vouchers, known as "swipes," to give other students free meals at campus dining halls. The program soon expanded to around 50 other schools. "Free dining passes have given me chances to eat when I thought I wouldn't be able to," said one student who took advantage of the program. "I used to go hungry and that would make it hard to focus in class or study. [The passes] really helped my studying and may have helped me get my GPA up" (Andrews 2018). Other universities attempted to address the problem of food insecurity on campus by redistributing leftover food from catered events, offering bagged meals for students to take home, or coordinating with student organizations or community groups to provide access to free food.

Other approaches to improving food security for college students involved increasing federal aid. The GAO report called upon federal lawmakers to expand the Supplemental Nutrition Assistance Program (SNAP), also known as food stamps, to cover more college students. The report estimated that nearly 2 million at-risk students were potentially eligible for SNAP in 2017 but did not receive benefits—usually because they lacked information about the program (Harris 2019a). In addition to creating outreach programs to inform students about SNAP, the GAO recommended clarifying eligibility requirements and relaxing rules that required most students to work at least 20 hours per week to qualify. Other policymakers suggested expanding the National School Lunch Program to include college students. "Students cannot solely rely on the generosity of food banks to keep on course to succeed," said U.S. Representative Jahana Hayes (D-CT). "We need to prioritize and address the systemic barriers in the way of an equitable path to a college degree" (Harris 2019b).

Some legislative proposals focused on expanding state and federal student aid to cover living expenses as well as tuition costs. Senator Patty

Murray (D-WA) sought to include this change as Congress worked on a reauthorization of the Higher Education Act. "Often we just talk about the tuition costs and dealing with that," she said. "It has to be broader than that—all of the costs that come to a student as they try to complete college, including food and housing" (Harris 2019a). Many of the proposals put forth by 2020 Democratic presidential candidates to make public college tuition free also included funding to cover college students' living expenses.

Conservative critics of these proposals expressed doubts about the prevalence of food insecurity on college campuses and opposed directing additional federal funds toward helping students afford higher education. In a controversial opinion piece for *USA Today*, James Bovard referred to surveys that found high rates of food insecurity among college students as "baloney," arguing that the results were compromised by design flaws, unrepresentative samples, and low response rates. Bovard also described "food insecurity" as a "vaporous term beloved by pro-welfare advocates." He cited statistics indicating that 70 percent of undergraduates gained weight during their college years, and that 41 percent qualified as overweight or obese by the time they graduated, as evidence that college students had plenty to eat (Bovard 2018).

Bovard concluded that federal education assistance provided more than enough money for college students to afford food, and he suggested that hungry students could solve the problem themselves by getting part-time jobs. "Many colleges would be wise to offer lower-price meal plans in lieu of the five-star buffets they serve," he wrote. "But a national goal of 'no college kid hungry' would bloat more students at a time when obesity wreaks more havoc than a few missed meals. In the long run, obliterating individuals' responsibility for feeding themselves is the worst possible dietary outcome" (Bovard 2018).

In 2019, Democrats in Congress introduced legislation intended to eliminate doubts about food and housing insecurity among college students by requiring federal agencies to collect data to measure the extent of these problems. The Closing the College Hunger Gap Act aimed to provide "a real, consistent national window on where student hunger is happening, where it's the worst, and [which] schools are creating interventions that make a difference," said Senator Chris Murphy (D-CT), one of the bill's sponsors (Harris 2019b). Armed with this information, institutions of higher learning could implement programs to increase affordability and access for nontraditional and low-income students. "Cost is the biggest reason why students do not enroll in or fail to complete college, far outstripping academic ability or performance," according to the Center for American Progress. "At many schools, particularly community colleges, the cost of nonacademic expenses—such as food, rent, and transportation—are far greater than the price of tuition and school fees. The result is that too often the dividing line between success and failure in American higher education is hunger, housing, and child care—not humanities, history, and calculus" (Postsecondary Education Team 2018).

Further Reading

Andrews, Michelle. 2018. "For Many College Students, Hunger Makes It 'Hard to Focus.'" NPR, July 31, 2018. https://www.npr.org/sections/health-shots/2018/07/31/634052183/for-many-college-students-hunger-makes-it-hard-to-focus.

Barboy, Dante. 2019. "What It Looks Like to Be Hungry in College." Center for American Progress, December 19, 2019. https://www.americanprogress.org/issues/education-postsecondary/news/2019/12/19/478916/looks-like-hungry-college/.

Bendix, Aria. 2017. "A Striking Number of College Students Are Hungry and Homeless." *Atlantic,* March 15, 2017. https://www.theatlantic.com/education/archive/2017/03/a-striking-number-of-college-students-are-hungry-and-homeless/519678/.

Bovard, James. 2018. "Starvation Problem in Universities? The Real College Problem Is Obesity." *USA Today,* April 11, 2018. https://www.usatoday.com/story/opinion/2018/04/11/obesity-not-starvation-real-problem-universities-column/500855002/.

College Board. 2019. "Trends in College Pricing Highlights." https://research.collegeboard.org/pdf/2019-trendsincp-highlights.pdf.

Goldrick-Rab, Sara, Jed Richardson, Joel Schneider, Anthony Hernandez, and Clare Cady. 2018. "Still Hungry and Homeless in College." Wisconsin HOPE Lab, April 2018. https://hope4college.com/wp-content/uploads/2018/09/Wisconsin-HOPE-Lab-Still-Hungry-and-Homeless.pdf.

Harris, Adam. 2019a. "Millions of College Students Are Going Hungry." *Atlantic,* January 9, 2019. https://www.theatlantic.com/education/archive/2019/01/college-student-hunger/579877/.

Harris, Adam. 2019b. "Many College Students Are Too Poor to Eat." *Atlantic,* July 11, 2019. https://www.theatlantic.com/education/archive/2019/07/lawmakers-introduce-bill-address-campus-hunger/593704/.

Hope Center. 2020. "College and University Basic Needs Insecurity: A #RealCollege Survey Report." Temple University, 2020. https://hope4college.com/college-and-university-basic-needs-insecurity-a-national-realcollege-survey-report/.

Laterman, Kaya. 2019. "Tuition or Dinner? Nearly Half of College Students Surveyed in a New Report Are Going Hungry." *New York Times,* May 2, 2019. https://www.nytimes.com/2019/05/02/nyregion/hunger-college-food-insecurity.html.

Nadworny, Elissa, and Clare Lombardo. 2019. "Report: College Students Are Hungry and Government Programs Could Do More to Help." NPR, January 10, 2019. https://www.npr.org/2019/01/10/683302685/report-college-students-are-hungry-and-government-programs-could-do-more-to-help.

Otero-Amad, Farah. 2019. "Hunger on Campus: The Fight against Student Food Insecurity." NBC News, December 1, 2019. https://www.nbcnews.com/news/us-news/hunger-campus-fight-against-student-food-insecurity-n1063291.

Postsecondary Education Team. 2018. "Beyond Tuition." Center for American Progress, June 20, 2018. https://www.americanprogress.org/issues/education-postsecondary/reports/2018/06/20/451899/beyond-tuition/.

Swipe Out Hunger. 2019. "The Evidence That #StudentHungerIsReal." https://www.swipehunger.org/the-evidence/.

Verbruggen, Robert. 2019. "College Students Are Not Starving." *National Review,* May 3, 2019. https://www.nationalreview.com/corner/college-students-are-not-starving/.

Proposals for Tuition-Free College

One approach to solving the college affordability crisis involves proposals to make college tuition-free or debt-free for all students with the necessary academic qualifications. Since Senator Bernie Sanders (I-VT) popularized this idea in his 2016 presidential campaign, many federal policymakers— as well as some state governments and charitable organizations—have developed their own plans to increase access to higher education by eliminating some or all costs to students and their families.

Proponents of free college programs argue that a bachelor's degree has become the minimum requirement for workers to succeed in the technology-driven twenty-first-century workplace, so it makes sense to extend the guarantee of free, universal public education beyond high school. They view free college as an investment that benefits society and the economy as well as increases educational and career opportunities for individuals. Opponents, however, contend that the individuals who benefit from higher education—rather than taxpayers—should be required to pay for it. "You have on the one hand a vision of higher education as part of a bundle of free (or at least very cheap) public services offered on equal terms to all—an extension of the principle of free high school," Matthew Yglesias explained in Vox. "Then you have on the other hand a vision of higher education as primarily a private benefit to students that should be financed through loans, with targeted assistance to particularly needy cases" (Yglesias 2019).

Free College Proposals

Free College for All formed the centerpiece of Sanders's bids for the Democratic presidential nomination in 2016 and 2020. "Every young person, regardless of their family income, the color of their skin, disability, or immigration status should have the opportunity to attend college," Sanders wrote on his campaign website. "Attending some of the best public colleges and universities was essentially free for students 50 years ago. Now, students are forced to pay upwards of $21,000 each year to attend those same schools" (Sanders 2020). Sanders pointed out that federal need-based financial aid had not kept up with rising college costs. Whereas an average student had to cover 25 percent of the total cost of attendance at a public university in the 1980s, by 2016 their share had risen to 56 percent (Nilsen 2019). As a result, many low-income students struggle with hunger and homelessness or accumulate massive debts to afford to attend college. "In the richest country in the history of the world, students should not have to starve in order to get an education," he declared (Sanders 2020). Although Sanders's presidential campaigns ultimately fell short, his focus on college affordability earned him enthusiastic support from young voters and helped pushed the issue to the forefront of political debate.

The proposals to eliminate college tuition advanced by Sanders and others vary in terms of which students qualify, which costs are covered, and which institutions participate. Most programs only apply to public nonprofit institutions, rather than private and for-profit colleges, because their funding is largely determined by state and federal appropriations. Some programs, such as one promoted by President Barack Obama before he left office in 2016, only eliminate tuition at two-year community colleges, while others apply to four-year institutions as well. Proposals for tuition-free college generally cover tuition and fees but not books, room and board, transportation, and other expenses. Proposals for debt-free college cover living expenses as well as tuition, but usually only for students with demonstrated financial need. More affluent students may be required to contribute to their own education costs to the extent that they can afford to do so without taking out student loans. So-called "first dollar" programs aim to cover the full costs of college by eliminating tuition and allowing students to receive additional grants and scholarships to pay living expenses. "Last dollar" programs, on the other hand, only cover the amount remaining after the student applies any need-based grants or merit-based scholarships. Finally, some programs restrict free tuition to low-income students, in-state students, first-time college students, or students who maintain good academic standing.

Free college proposals also differ in terms of estimated costs and sources of funding. Paying for college for up to 20 million undergraduate students nationwide is an expensive proposition, with estimates for different programs ranging from $50 billion to $100 billion per year (Whistle and Hiler 2019). The funding mechanism for Sanders's plan involved imposing a financial transactions tax on stock trades. Senator Elizabeth Warren (D-MA) proposed funding her free college and student debt forgiveness plans by charging a wealth tax on the richest 0.1 percent of Americans, or households worth $50 million or more. Senator Brian Schatz (D-HI) and Representative Mark Pocan (D-WI) introduced a $95 billion debt-free college package that aimed to help low-income students pay the full cost of college, including living expenses and books, without taking out loans. "Covering tuition for everybody is not a bad idea—it's just that tuition is only 45 percent of the cost of college," Schatz explained. "I also believe that we ought to cover the full cost of college for people who can't afford it before we cover tuition for people who can" (Nilsen 2019).

Most of these proposals used federal funds to create incentives for states to increase their appropriations for public colleges and universities. Sanders's plan offered two-to-one federal matching grants to states that increased their higher education funding by enough to eliminate tuition for students at public universities. Warren's plan declared that "the federal government will partner with states to split the costs of tuition and fees and ensure that states maintain their current levels of funding on need-based financial aid and academic instruction" (Yglesias 2019). Schatz and Pocan's bill offered a dollar-for-dollar federal match for state grants to cover the full cost of college for students with financial need. If all 50 states chose to participate, Schatz estimated that 10 states could make public university attendance debt-free for all students within a year, while 22 states could provide debt-free public college for low-income students eligible for federal Pell Grants (Nilsen 2019).

Criticism and Alternative Approaches

Critics contend, however, that the incentives offered under most free college proposals would not convince many states to participate. Since states bear the primary responsibility for organizing and funding their own public higher education systems, such proposals would require state buy-in to be effective. "Regardless of what happens in presidential politics, the success or failure of the free college movement is ultimately bound to be determined in the states—where most legislative houses remain firmly under GOP control," wrote Yglesias (2019). Many states reduced their levels of funding for higher education in the wake of the 2008 recession. By 2017, overall state funding for public two- and four-year colleges had declined by $9 billion from a decade earlier (Nilsen 2019). State disinvestment contributed to increases in tuition rates and rising student debt levels, as colleges adjusted to the loss of revenue by shifting more of the costs to students. If the federal government increased education funding without state cooperation, therefore, some critics worry it would lead to even higher college costs. "The basic reality is that the federal government does not run colleges or universities and does not set tuition or spending levels at colleges or universities," wrote Yglesias. "Consequently, this whole space is stalked by the fear that if the federal government makes an open-ended commitment to cover students' tuition, states will simply allow college spending to soar" (Yglesias 2019).

Critics of tuition-free or debt-free college plans also assert that they benefit affluent students more than low-income students and thus amount to a regressive use of government funds. Proponents note that all higher education spending—free college programs included—tends to benefit wealthier families because their children are statistically more likely to attend college. Children from affluent families are also likely to attend more expensive four-year institutions and pay higher tuition rates than children from low-income families, who often attend less pricey two-year community colleges and receive Pell Grants and other need-based financial aid to offset tuition costs. As a result of these factors, critics claim that programs eliminating tuition could increase economic inequality. "There are all sorts of increases in education spending I'd support for the sake of equality of opportunity," Conor Friedersdorf wrote in the *Atlantic*. "But the notion that *all students* should pay *nothing* for college is preposterous. It would've been scandalous for me to get a four-year education for free in a state [California] with homeless people living on the streets, desperately poor immigrants working 363 days a year as day laborers, crumbling infrastructure, and a very near future with multiple cities literally going bankrupt" (Friedersdorf 2013).

Economists from the Urban Institute who reviewed Warren's free college plan estimated that families with household incomes over $120,000 per year would receive 38 percent of the benefits, while families earning less than $35,000 per year would only receive 8 percent (Weissmann 2019). Their analysis only included full-time undergraduates, however, even though part-time students comprise 40 percent of all collegegoers and would also benefit. In addition, the analysts did not consider that Warren's plan allows low-income students to apply their need-based financial aid toward living expenses after their tuition costs are covered, which helps equalize the benefits.

Other critics argue that free-tuition programs would encourage more high-income students to choose public universities rather than private colleges, thus increasing the competition for limited spots. One study suggested that up to 20 percent of low-income students could end up being "crowded out" of selective four-year public universities if tuition were eliminated (Whistle and Hiler 2019). Many of these students would be diverted to two-year community colleges, which would decrease their chances of completing a bachelor's degree by 18 percent. Since people with two-year associate's degrees earn $14,000 less per year, on average, than people with four-year bachelor's degrees, this outcome could also perpetuate income inequality (Whistle and Hiler 2019). Some proponents of free college suggest limiting the program to community colleges and covering the full cost of a two-year degree for all students. They claim that this option would be less expensive and less complicated to administer than larger plans but provide significant benefits to low-income students.

Some critics object to the idea of free college because higher education offers significant financial benefits to individuals. Pete Buttigieg, a 2020 Democratic presidential candidate and former mayor of South Bend, Indiana, rejected the free college plans offered by his rivals. Buttigieg took out student loans to finance his own studies at Harvard, and he viewed higher education as an investment that paid off in higher future earnings. He suggested reserving free-tuition programs for students with family incomes under $100,000 and proposed increasing the maximum federal Pell Grant amount to cover living expenses for students with financial need. "As a progressive, I have a hard time getting my head around the idea of a majority who earn less because they didn't go to college subsidizing a minority who earn more because they did," he remarked (Weissmann 2019).

Many commentators support increasing the maximum Pell Grant from $6,345 at the beginning of the 2020-2021 academic year to double or even triple that amount. They point out that the Pell Grant covers less than one-third of the cost of attendance at public four-year institutions—leaving low-income students with $17.8 billion in unmet financial need—whereas it once covered 80 percent of the costs. Given the high price tags of most free college proposals, proponents note that the federal government could use those funds to triple the maximum Pell Grant amount for existing recipients or to give the current maximum Pell Grant to an additional 16 million students per year (Whistle and Hiler 2019). Other supporters of free college programs, however, point out that the federal government already spends more than $90 billion per year to subsidize higher education through need-based aid, tax benefits, and student loan interest payments for people currently enrolled in college. They argue that eliminating Pell Grants and other subsidies would free up enough money to fully fund most free college proposals (Duggan 2020).

Another alternative to free college programs involves allowing students to earn a higher education subsidy by volunteering to participate in a national service program, such as Americorps. Proponents claim that an "earned college" program would encourage young people to give back to their communities as well as provide them with funds to pay college expenses. Public opinion polls showed higher approval rates for such programs among likely voters than for free college plans (Whistle and Hiler 2019). A Quinnipiac University survey, for instance, found that 52 percent of voters opposed making all public U.S. colleges and universities free, while 45 percent favored the idea. The results highlighted generational differences in support for free college, however, with 61 percent of voters between ages 18 and 34 backing such plans (Smith 2019). "To older voters, accustomed to the cheap college tuition that prevailed decades ago, 'free college' sounds quixotic and frivolous," Yglesias explained. "To younger people burdened by today's much higher tuition structure and loan-based financing system, it's a clear commitment to fix a broken system" (Yglesias 2019).

To some proponents of free college, the concept represents a government commitment to securing the right to higher education for all Americans. "To guarantee free college to qualified students is a way of saying that higher education is important and valued, which is one reason the idea seems very popular among young college graduates who would not actually benefit in a concrete way," Yglesias noted (2019). Although free college benefits all students—including those with family incomes high enough to pay tuition—some supporters argue that promoting college affordability and access for everyone would increase public acceptance of the programs. "Letting everybody enjoy nice things like higher education for free or cheap creates buy-in for a robust welfare state, whereas programs for the poor are easily targeted for cuts," Jordan Weissmann wrote in Slate. "It's not just about helping the poorest kids afford school. It's about establishing the idea that certain things, like education at every level, are a right, and building support for strong public institutions to provide them" (Weissmann 2019).

Further Reading

Duggan, Cherone. 2020. "Could College Be Free?" *Harvard Magazine,* January-February 2020. https://harvardmagazine.com/2020/01/free-college-deming.

Friedersdorf, Conor. 2013. "Universal Free College Would Be a Regressive Scandal." *Atlantic,* July 30, 2013. https://www.theatlantic.com/politics/archive/2013/07/universal-free-college-would-be-a-regressive-scandal/278201/.

McHarris, Philip V., and Zellie Imani. 2020. "It Is Time to Cancel Student Debt and Make Higher Education Free." *Al Jazeera,* April 26, 2020. https://www.aljazeera.com/indepth/opinion/time-cancel-student-debt-higher-education-free-200425104050766.html.

Nilsen, Emma. 2019. "Progressives Want to Go Further Than Tuition-Free College—Here's Their Proposal to Make It Debt-Free." Vox, March 7, 2019. https://www.vox.com/2019/3/7/18252270/progressives-tuition-debt-free-college-schatz-pocan.

Sanders, Bernie. 2020. "Issues: College for All and Cancel All Student Debt." https://berniesanders.com/issues/free-college-cancel-debt/.

Smith, Ashley A. 2019. "Poll: Voters Oppose Free College, Loan Forgiveness." *Inside Higher Ed,* May 1, 2019. https://www.insidehighered.com/quicktakes/2019/05/01/poll-voters-oppose-free-college-loan-forgiveness.

Taylor, Astra. 2020. "Cancelling Student Debt Was Always the Right Thing to Do. Now It's Imperative." *Guardian,* April 7, 2020. https://www.theguardian.com/commentisfree/2020/apr/07/cancel-student-debt-coronavirus.

Weissmann, Jordan. 2019. "Critics Complain That Free College Wouldn't Be Progressive. They're Missing the Point." Slate, May 6, 2019. https://slate.com/business/2019/05/free-college-tuition-warren-sanders.html.

Whistle, Wesley, and Tamara Hiler. 2019. "Why Free College Could Increase Inequality." Third Way, March 19, 2019. https://www.thirdway.org/memo/why-free-college-could-increase-inequality.

Yglesias, Matthew. 2019. "Democrats' Ongoing Argument about Free College, Explained." Vox, June 24, 2019. https://www.vox.com/2019/6/24/18677785/democrats-free-college-sanders-warren-biden.

Student Debt and the U.S. Economy

Many young people view earning a college degree as a necessary step toward getting ahead in the competitive environment of the twenty-first-century workforce. As the costs of higher education increased at more than double the rate of inflation, however, a growing number of students had to rely upon loans to afford college. By 2019, an estimated 45 million Americans held a total of $1.6 trillion in student debt. This figure represented about 8 percent of total annual personal income in the United States, and it ranked below only home mortgages—and above automobile loans and credit card balances—as a source of household debt obligation (Ingraham 2019).

Facing an average outstanding loan balance of more than $37,000, many borrowers struggled under the financial burden for decades. The high monthly payments—sometimes compounded by steep penalties and interest—forced them to delay or forego discretionary consumer spending that drives economic growth. Some analysts portrayed the rapid rise in student debt as a crisis, asserting that it harmed borrowers and their families, increased the risk of recession, and even threatened to disrupt the U.S. sociopolitical order. "It doesn't take an economist to see that America's future generations have been handed an albatross to wear along with their caps and gowns," John E. Girouard wrote in *Forbes*. "But of course that albatross isn't just the students' problem—it could well be the next crisis that could strangle the American economy" (Girouard 2018).

Putting the American Dream on Hold

For the 70 percent of students who must borrow money to afford college, student loan debt affects many decisions made after graduation. "If you've never had student loans, it may be hard to understand what it feels like to be so financially burdened before you've even earned your first paycheck," Girouard wrote. "It's terrifying" (Girouard 2018). In one survey of recent graduates, 86 percent cited student debt as a significant source of stress (Brink Editorial Staff 2019). The need to repay loans caused some degree earners to be less selective in the job market. "They are more inclined to accept part-time work and jobs that are less related to their degree and offer limited career potential," according to one study (Ingraham 2019). U.S. Representative Alexandria Ocasio-Cortez (D-NY), for instance, famously worked as a bartender after she graduated from Boston University in 2011 with a dual degree in economics and international relations, along with $27,000 in student debt. Anger over the limited life choices available to members of the millennial generation propelled her successful campaign to become the youngest woman ever elected to Congress in 2018.

Carrying mountains of student debt closed off certain career paths for recent college graduates. Many young entrepreneurs abandoned dreams of starting their own businesses, for example, due to shaky credit scores and a lack of seed money. One study found that small business formation declined by 14 percent—the equivalent of 70 new businesses per county—for every one standard deviation increase in student debt. Since small businesses accounted for an estimated 60 percent of employment growth, this decline had negative repercussions for the U.S. economy. "There's a lot of business activity that isn't taking place," said economics professor Barbara O'Neill. "It's a drag on everything" (Ingraham 2019). Many college graduates with large debt burdens also discarded plans to pursue careers in the nonprofit or public-service sectors—such as teaching, nursing, or social work—since those jobs tended to pay less than comparable positions in the private sector.

Student debt also influenced personal life decisions for many college graduates, often forcing them to postpone such milestones as getting married and having children. Among women who earned bachelor's degrees, for instance, research showed that the odds of marriage in the four years after graduation decreased by 2 percent per month for every $1,000 increase in student loan debt (Ingraham 2019). In another survey, 19 percent of borrowers reported delaying marriage due to student debt, while 26 percent said they put off starting a family (Brink Editorial Staff 2019). "A lot of things are being postponed," O'Neill stated. "You got what you call a crowding-out effect—people only have so much money" (Ingraham 2019).

Hefty student loan payments also prevented many young people from saving money for a down payment or qualifying for a mortgage, which contributed to a significant drop in homeownership rates. According to the Urban Institute, homeownership among recent college graduates declined by 15 percent for every 1 percent increase in student loan debt. As a result, only 37 percent of millennials purchased their first home by the age of 30, compared to 45 percent of members of earlier generations (Girouard 2018). Declining homeownership impacted the economy by limiting new home construction and restricting sales of existing homes. "And home ownership *now* is just one part of the equation—what happens when folks who haven't been able to buy real estate fall on hard times in retirement?" Girouard noted. "There will be no large asset to sell, no 'downsizing' to be done, no reverse mortgage to the rescue" (Girouard 2018).

Student debt also posed a threat to borrowers' short-term and long-term financial security. A Federal Reserve report noted that households with student debt had a median net worth less than half that of households without student debt (Ingraham 2019). As a result, young people who struggled to repay student loans lacked discretionary income to spend on goods and services or to save for retirement. Some experts claimed that lower spending by a generation of indebted college graduates contributed to a 1 to 2 percent decline in the U.S. gross national product. "Because student loan debt is a drag on household spending, the ability for those with student loan debt to consume in the economy is diminished," Robert Farrington explained in *Forbes*. "They cannot buy housing, vehicles, or spend on consumer goods. Their ability to participate in the financial markets (i.e. invest) will be limited. All of these factors will have a negative trend on the economy—and it will happen over the long run" (Farrington 2018).

In addition to limiting the purchasing power of a generation of American consumers, massive student loan debt posed a threat to borrowers, financial institutions, and taxpayers due to the risk of default. As of 2018, around one million borrowers went into default on their federally guaranteed student loans each year, and experts predicted that up to 40 percent of all borrowers could enter default by 2023. The risk disproportionately affected women and minorities, who tended to take on higher debt loads in college and to earn lower salaries once they entered the workforce. For instance, the default rate for black bachelor's degree recipients, at 21 percent, was 5 times higher than for white graduates (Nova 2018). The combination of loan defaults and loan forgiveness extended to victims of for-profit college scams cost the federal government—and American taxpayers—an estimated $170 billion per year. "It's a slow but steady sinkhole that is quietly gobbling up any hope for sustainable long-term growth in the U.S. economy," Girouard declared (Girouard 2018).

Limiting the Damage to the U.S. Economy

Some analysts downplayed the student debt crisis and its impact on the U.S. economy. Despite the rising costs of college, they insisted that higher education remained a solid investment in the future for most students. They pointed out that college graduates, on average, earned higher incomes over their lifetimes and contributed to economic growth by spending money and paying taxes. Yet other experts questioned conventional wisdom about the value of higher education. They argued that skyrocketing tuition rates, coupled with stagnant starting salaries for degree earners, forced a growing number of students to take out loans they would struggle for decades to pay back. Mike Calhoun, president of the Center for Responsible Lending, cited the "mismatch between the debt and the borrower's income, their ability to repay," as the foundation of an impending financial crisis that "will affect tens of millions of families" (Arnold 2019).

Calhoun and other economists drew parallels between the student debt crisis and the subprime mortgage housing bubble that "popped" in 2007 and sent the U.S. economy spiraling into a major recession. They claimed that federal government guarantees on student loans encouraged private lenders to engage in irresponsible lending practices that disregarded borrowers' ability to repay. They also noted that some Wall Street investment firms created a speculative market for student loan obligations, which carried inherent risk as a form of debt unsecured by physical collateral. Although some economists predicted that high default rates on student loans could trigger a sudden financial crisis and economic downturn, others argued that the effects would be gradual and long lasting. "The collateral that backs student loan debt is the borrower's future earnings," Farrington explained. "As long as there is earning potential, the ability to have the loans quickly 'pop' via any financial mechanism is rare.... The net effect of this student loan crisis won't be a bubble popping—it will be [a] slow drag on the economy. And it's an anchor that's already taking hold and pulling back the American economy from what it could be" (Farrington 2018).

Members of the millennial generation saw their futures shaped by the financial crisis and recession, which left many college graduates facing poor employment prospects and large student loan debts. Anger, frustration, and concerns about their financial security caused many young people to question the feasibility of the American dream. Some millennials expressed support for democratic socialists such as Ocasio-Cortez and Senator Bernie Sanders (I-VT), who demanded an overhaul of the nation's basic political and economic systems to promote fairness and reduce income inequality. A 2019 NBC News/*Wall Street Journal* poll revealed that millennials (defined as being between the ages of 18 and 34) held more positive views of socialism than any other group of Americans. Only 38 percent reported negative feelings, while 62 percent said they felt positive, neutral, or undecided (Chinni and Bronston 2019). Although younger voters typically hold more liberal views than older voters, some analysts attributed the growing support for socialism to disillusionment with the capitalist system. "After sinking a big down payment into their education, many millennials are finding themselves with piles of debt and no easy way to buy into the American dream," according to NBC News. "That may be leaving some of them with mixed feelings about the economic system as it currently functions and perhaps more hungry for dramatic changes in how it operates" (Chinni and Bronston 2019).

Economists proposed a wide range of changes aimed at resolving the student debt crisis and limiting its impact on the U.S. economy. Some proposals focused on lowering college costs, which would address the root of the problem by reducing the need for students to borrow money to earn a degree. Critics asserted that colleges could reduce tuition costs by cutting administrative staff positions and salaries, providing fewer amenities, and embracing technology for online learning. Other proposals called for helping prospective college students choose affordable alternatives, understand the consequences of borrowing, and avoid incurring more debt than their eventual income would support. Some economists also suggested cracking down on fraudulent for-profit colleges and unscrupulous private lenders that preyed upon low-income students and accounted for a large share of loan defaults.

Many proposals to alleviate the student debt crisis sought to help borrowers make payments or to reduce or cancel their outstanding loan balances. Some analysts recommended that the federal government lower interest rates on student loans, simplify and promote income-based repayment options, and expand incentives such as the Public Service Loan Forgiveness Program. Others suggested offering tax credits to help parents pay education expenses or tax deductions to help students pay tuition. One proposal allowed businesses to help employees repay their education loans by counting loan payments as tax-deductible 401(k) contributions and making them eligible for employer matching funds. Finally, several 2020 Democratic presidential candidates included student loan forgiveness in their campaign platforms. Senator Elizabeth Warren (D-MA), for instance, promised to immediately cancel up to $50,000 in federal loans for 42 million Americans. Warren argued that eliminating student debt would "provide an enormous middle-class stimulus that will boost economic growth, increase home purchases, and fuel a new wave of small business formation" (Warren 2020).

Without taking steps to address the problem, the student debt crisis appeared likely to impact the U.S. economy far into the future. Some economists predicted that the total outstanding student loan debt would double to reach $3 trillion by 2030 (Johnson 2019). Measures to alleviate student debt, on the other hand, had the potential to benefit more than struggling borrowers. "Remember that the better everyone's standard of living, the more money our country has to run," Girouard wrote. "It's always been this country's bread and butter to have citizens with money to earn, money to spend, and money with which to pay Uncle Sam. It's time we took steps to ensure that more Americans—*educated* Americans—are set up to become fuel for tomorrow's economy rather than a drain on it" (Girouard 2018).

Further Reading

Arnold, Chris. 2019. "Student Loans a Lot Like the Subprime Mortgage Debacle, Watchdog Says." NPR, December 9, 2019. https://www.npr.org/2019/12/09/785527874/student-loans-a-lot-like-the-subprime-mortgage-debacle-watchdog-says.

Brink Editorial Staff. 2019. "Is Student Debt Dragging Down the U.S. Economy?" Brink, August 22, 2019. https://www.brinknews.com/is-student-debt-dragging-down-the-u-s-economy/.

Chinni, Dante, and Sally Bronston. 2019. "The Real College Crisis: Student Debt Drags Down Economy." NBC News, March 17, 2019. https://www.nbcnews.com/politics/meet-the-press/real-college-crisis-student-debt-drags-down-economy-n984131.

Farrington, Robert. 2018. "Why the Student Loan Bubble Won't Burst." *Forbes,* December 12, 2018. https://www.forbes.com/sites/robertfarrington/2018/12/12/student-loan-bubble-wont-burst/#594682156768.

Girouard, John E. 2018. "How Student Debt Is Destroying the Economy and How We Can Stop It in Its Tracks." *Forbes,* November 8, 2018. https://www.forbes.com/sites/investor/2018/11/08/how-student-debt-is-destroying-the-economy-and-how-we-can-stop-it-in-its-tracks/#15f2fa796619.

Healey, Patrick B. 2019. "We Should All Be Concerned about the Student Debt Crisis." CNBC, November 4, 2019. https://www.cnbc.com/2019/11/04/we-should-all-be-concerned-about-the-student-debt-crisis.html.

Ingraham, Christopher. 2019. "Seven Ways $1.6 Trillion in Student Loan Debt Affects the U.S. Economy." *Washington Post,* June 25, 2019. https://www.washingtonpost.com/business/2019/06/25/heres-what-trillion-student-loan-debt-is-doing-us-economy/.

Johnson, Daniel M. 2019. "What Will It Take to Solve the Student Loan Crisis?" *Harvard Business Review,* September 23, 2019. https://hbr.org/2019/09/what-will-it-take-to-solve-the-student-loan-crisis.

Nova, Annie. 2018. "More Than One Million People Default on Their Student Loans Each Year." CNBC, August 13, 2018. https://www.cnbc.com/2018/08/13/twenty-two-percent-of-student-loan-borrowers-fall-into-default.html.

Warren, Elizabeth. 2020. "Affordable Higher Education for All." https://elizabethwarren.com/plans/affordable-higher-education.

Zaloom, Caitlin. 2019. *Indebted: How Families Make College Work at Any Cost.* Princeton, NJ: Princeton University Press.

Student Loan Debt and Individual Borrowers

The total student debt outstanding in the United States tripled between 2005 and 2020 to reach an estimated $1.6 trillion—an amount greater than the annual gross domestic product of all but a dozen countries. As more Americans came to view higher education as necessary to achieve a comfortable standard of living, rapidly rising tuition rates forced an increasing number of students to rely upon borrowing to pay for college. Federal policies encouraged students to take on debt to finance higher education by loosening lending rules, increasing the maximum amounts students could borrow, eliminating income limits for loan eligibility, and establishing programs to enable parents to obtain education loans.

As wages stagnated, however, some borrowers found themselves saddled with unmanageable levels of debt for years or even decades after leaving college. Many borrowers reported that the struggle to repay student loans shaped their life decisions, contributed to financial insecurity, and caused severe emotional distress. "We've essentially engaged in a failed social experiment where the government thought that it would be fine to give people student debt because that would pay off in the long run, and we're seeing that's not the case," said Roosevelt Institute researcher Julie Margetta-Morgan. "Individuals shouldn't bear all the burden for paying for that mistake" (Berman 2018).

The Student Debt Burden

Among students who completed undergraduate degrees in 2018, around 70 percent held student loans, with an average outstanding balance of about $30,000. Students who attended public universities typically owed slightly less than average, while students who attended private nonprofit colleges typically owed slightly more. Students who attended for-profit institutions carried the heaviest undergraduate debt loads, with half owing more than $40,000. Still, the amount of debt accumulated by undergraduate students paled in comparison with the amount borrowed by graduate students. In fact, people who earned advanced degrees accounted for half of the $1.6 trillion in outstanding student loan debt, even though they only comprised 25 percent of bor-rowers. While some of the most distressing stories concerned borrowers whose debt burdens reach six figures, only 6 percent of borrowers owed more than $100,000 (Looney, Wessel, and Yilla 2020).

Statistics indicated that certain borrowers were more likely to struggle to repay student debt than others. People who took out student loans but then left college without completing a degree, for instance, incurred debt without receiving the career benefits that typically accompanied education credentials. "The people having problems with their debts are those who dropped out of school after just a few courses or a year," noted University of Michigan economist Susan Dynarski. One study found that 3.9 million undergraduates with student loans dropped out of college between 2014 and 2016. Students who quit before finishing a degree ended up defaulting on their loans three times more often than those who earned a diploma (Nadworny and Lombardo 2019). Ashlee, a woman from Kentucky, entered college in 2010 but dropped out during her third year when work and family demands became overwhelming. She eventually defaulted on $12,000 in student loans, and with penal-ties and interest she wound up owing more than she initially borrowed. "I'm drowning in debt for a piece of paper I never received," Ashlee stated. "Nobody should be in this position" (Nadworny and Lombardo 2019).

Students who attended for-profit colleges also tended to struggle to repay their loans. Unlike public and private nonprofit institutions, which reinvested tuition income in facilities and instruction to benefit students, for-profit education providers operated as businesses with an imperative to generate profits for investors. Although for-profit schools typically charged higher tuition rates than comparable nonprofit institutions, they targeted a student demographic that was eligible for need-based federal financial aid and encouraged them to borrow money to cover the cost. As a result, 96 percent of students at for-profit schools took out student loans, compared to 13 percent at community colleges. Critics charged that for-profit colleges failed to deliver quality instruction, so many students either dropped out or received useless degrees that did not improve their employment opportunities. Dynarski described the educational outcomes for most for-profit college students as "little education, lots of debt" (Nadworny 2019).

Default rates for students who attended for-profit colleges were nearly double the rates for students who attended community college. In fact, although for-profit schools accounted for only 10 percent of total college enrollment, for-profit attendees accounted for nearly half of all defaults on student loans (HELP 2012). Shawn, a Philadelphia resident who took graphic design classes at for-profit ITT Technical Institute until the school closed, ended up defaulting on his $12,000 in student loans. "I feel like I'm stuck in quicksand," he noted. "I can't finance a car and can't get a credit card" (Nadworny and Lombardo 2019). Given the high default rates among students who attended for-profit institutions, some critics called on policymakers to stop supplying taxpayer funds to the for-profit education industry. "The government has been lending a lot of money to students who went to low-quality programs that they didn't complete, or that didn't help them get a well-paying job, or were outright frauds," wrote the authors of a Brookings Institution report. "One obvious solution: Stop lending money to encourage students to attend such schools" (Looney, Wessel, and Yilla 2020).

Researchers also noted racial disparities in student debt burdens and default rates. African American students tended to borrow more than their white peers due to lower levels of family income and generational wealth. In addition, black students were more likely to attend for-profit colleges, which entailed higher tuition rates and student loan amounts. After graduation, black workers often received lower salaries than their white counterparts. As a result of these factors, 38 percent of black students who entered college in 2003-2004 defaulted on their student loans within 12 years, compared to 12 percent of white students. The racial disparity still held true among bachelor's degree recipients, with black college graduates defaulting at five times the rate of white graduates, 21 percent to 4 percent (Looney,

Wessel, and Yilla 2020). "In other words, the bachelor's degree can't completely wipe away issues related to race," said Ben Miller of the Center for American Progress (Nadworny 2019).

Studies also found higher default rates among students from low-income families. Students who received need-based federal Pell Grants and also took out federal loans were more likely to default than higher-income students. The precarious financial security of low-income students meant that any unanticipated expense could cause difficulty making loan payments, which raised the potential for default even if the outstanding debt amount was relatively small. "If you look at the likelihood that someone is going to default, it actually drops as debt goes up," Dynarski explained. "That sounds completely counterintuitive, but that's because the missing piece here is earnings. You can't pay off a debt if you don't have any money" (Nadworny and Lombardo 2019). As a result, the borrowers most likely to default held less than $10,000 in student loan debt (Nadworny 2019).

Due to increases in parental borrowing, greater numbers of nontraditional students seeking college degrees after spending many years in the workforce, and lengthening of loan terms, many older Americans also struggle to repay education debt. Researchers found that the average amount of education loans taken out by parents tripled between 1995 and 2020, and that nearly 9 percent of parent borrowers owed more than $100,000 (Looney, Wessel, and Yilla 2020). Studies also showed that student loan debt weighed heavily on many households headed by older Americans, affecting 29 percent of families headed by someone between ages 55 and 64, and 13 percent of families headed by someone between 65 and 74 (Valenti, Edelman, and Van Ostern 2013). According to a report published by American Student Assistance, "student debt is an issue not only for the young, but also for the young at heart—recent graduates of all ages, middle-aged adults with loans from their own education or that of a family member, and an increasing population of seniors struggling with student loans into their retirement years." Furthermore, "paying back college loans now often intersects with both paying for a child's higher education and saving for retirement, leaving many seniors cash-strapped long after their senior year of college has become a distant memory" (American Student Assistance 2017).

Some critics claim that federal programs intended to alleviate student debt burdens and reduce default rates—such as income-driven repayment plans, deferment options, and consolidation loans—mainly extended the period of time for borrowers to be indebted. Although most federal loans originated with a standard 10-year term, studies showed that more than half of all borrowers extended that term. As a result, the average time required to repay a federal student loan nearly doubled between 2000 and 2017. "Extending payments for up to 25 years could mean the borrower will pay much more over time and be saddled with a student loan bill into their 40s and 50s," according to American Student Assistance (2017). For an increasing number of older Americans, the student debt obligation followed them into retirement. In 2015, more than 173,000 recipients of Social Security retirement, disability, or survivor benefits saw them garnished for student loan payments. Student loans were the only type of debt allowed to be collected from Social Security, as well as the only type not dischargeable through bankruptcy. "The reality for hundreds of thousands of seniors is a monthly struggle to pay for education, intended to improve their lives and economic wellbeing, long after that career benefit has subsided" (American Student Assistance 2017).

Impacts on Borrowers' Lives

Lawmakers initially envisioned federal student loans as a means of enabling young Americans to invest in their own financial futures. Loans provided access to college—and a pathway to better jobs and a more comfortable life—for students who might otherwise struggle to afford it. As more students incurred higher levels of debt to pay rising tuition rates, however, critics questioned whether the system paid off in terms of borrowers' future prosperity and happiness. "We are making several policy decisions right now based on the idea that student debt is essentially a benign mechanism for funding higher education," Margetta-Morgan noted. "Our research suggests that is not, in fact, that case" (Berman 2018). Instead, surveys revealed that student loan debt often had negative impacts on borrowers for decades after they left college. "People with student loan debt are carrying a serious financial and emotional burden," said Tim DeMello of Gradifi, a company that helped employers create student loan benefits for employees. "The pressure of making big monthly loan payments is taking its toll in terms of stress, housing affordability, and quality of life" (Dickler 2017).

A 2018 survey by the nonprofit group Student Debt Crisis collected information about the experiences of 7,095 borrowers in all 50 states. The respondents carried an average outstanding student loan balance of $87,500—more than twice the national average—and earned incomes of around $60,000 per year. Many respondents reported that their student debt burden forced them to delay or forego major life milestones. For example, 19 percent said it made them wait to get married, 26 percent said it made them put off having children, and 56 percent said it interfered with their plans to purchase a home. "We are waiting to have children and buy a home because our combined student debt is more than a mortgage on a home," Maine resident Sean said of himself and his wife. "I often imagine what life would look like for us if we were not imprisoned by debt to our current life" (Hembree 2018). Student debt obligations also forced many young people to return to the family home after completing college and to depend on their parents for financial support.

Student debt also contributed to financial insecurity for many borrowers. The Student Debt Crisis survey found that the majority of respondents had less than $1,000 in their bank accounts. In addition, many borrowers reported that their student loan payments were higher than their monthly expenses for rent (33 percent), health insurance (56 percent), or food (65 percent). Eighty percent of respondents said repaying student loans made it impossible for them to save for retirement (Hembree 2018). As a result, one study found that college-educated married couples with student debt accumulated $200,000 less wealth, on average, than couples who were able to invest their money (Zaloom 2019, 185). "These survey results reveal that student loan borrowers are on thin ice, and many are falling through without a lifeline," said Will Sealy of Summer, a company that helps borrowers repay their student loans. "That means that millions of Americans face financial calamity, with all the limitations and stress that comes with it" (Hembree 2018).

Many borrowers reported that struggling to repay student debt affected their physical and mental health. More than 85 percent cited student debt as a significant source of stress, while one-third described it as the biggest source of stress in their lives. "My student loans have prevented me from really living," said Colleen, a borrower from Pennsylvania. "They stress me out more than I can explain. I pay and pay and pay, and the balance never seems to go down. . . . It's frustrating and honestly makes me feel completely defeated" (Hembree 2018). A survey of 1,000 borrowers conducted by the informational website Student Loan Hero found associations between student debt-related stress and mental health issues, including anxiety, depression, irritability, and substance abuse. More than half of the borrowers surveyed also reported experiencing physical symptoms of stress, such as headaches (71 percent), insomnia (64 percent), muscle tension (56 percent), and upset stomach (50 percent) (Insler 2017). "We do get stories of borrowers who are struggling with the idea of suicide," noted Natalia Abrams of Student Debt Crisis. "These are not people who tried to get rich quick; these are not people looking for a handout" (Hembree 2018).

Some borrowers sought deferments or other assistance from their loan servicers—financial services companies that operate under contract with the Department of Education—only to receive inaccurate information and be subjected to interest and fees. Nearly 60 percent of borrowers surveyed by Student Debt Crisis said they received "confusing" or "unhelpful" advice from their loan servicer. In addition, 42 percent said they had trouble negotiating changes to their repayment terms during financial hardships, and 25 percent recalled being charged excess fees. "I have begged multiple times for Sallie Mae to assist in lowering the monthly payments when a medical event happens, to which they have told me to quit my job and find a better-paying one," said borrower Melissa of Texas. "Regularly, I contemplate selling everything and living in my car to help free up money to pay off the debt sooner" (Hembree 2018).

Borrowers who struggled to make payments on their student loans often experienced harassment from loan servicers and collection agencies. They had little recourse, however, since student loans were not subject to the standard consumer protections that applied to other types of debts. Maryland resident Kenneth Newsome saw his $9,500 in student debt balloon to $36,000 after he requested a deferment to deal with a family health crisis. The Department of Education also rejected his application for loan relief as a teacher in an urban school district. "I have paid the amount I owe twice," he declared in a statement on the Student Debt Crisis website. "I am being extorted by these companies by them doubling what I owe and increasing the amounts I owe when they either sell my loan or increase the interest rates to a high amount. My life has been delayed and I'm getting no younger. Stop playing with people like me. Stop living high on the hog off of people like me" (Newsome 2020).

Recognizing the potential for student loan-based stress to negatively impact employees' morale and productivity, an increasing number of companies began offering benefit programs aimed at helping employees manage and pay down their debts. Some businesses provided direct monthly loan payments on behalf of employees, while others offered to make contributions to employees' 401(k) retirement accounts to match their student loan payments. A few companies allowed employees to trade paid vacation days or holidays for student loan assistance. Companies such as Aetna, Fidelity, Hulu, PwC, and Random House noted that these benefit programs aided in their recruiting and retention of employees. One study found that 90 percent of workers with student loans preferred to work for a company that offered repayment assistance (Dickler 2017), while a Society for Human Resource Management survey ranked student loan programs second behind paid time off among the benefits most valued by young employees (MacLellan 2019). A $100 monthly employer contribution, for instance, allowed a borrower with a loan balance of $26,500 at

4 percent interest to save shave three years off the 10-year term and save $10,000 (Dickler 2017).

To alleviate the student debt crisis and its wide-ranging effects, some policymakers suggested forgiving all outstanding student loans. Other experts recommended overhauling the U.S. college finance system to lift the burden off of students and their families. "Student debt burdens too many families and students," anthropologist Caitlin Zaloom wrote in *Indebted*. "The financial systems we've developed for helping students and families get access to higher education do far more harm than is necessary, and introduce too many difficult tensions into family life.... We need a new system that genuinely supports families and creates more opportunity" (Zaloom 2019, 200).

Further Reading

American Student Assistance. 2017. *Retirement Delayed: The Impact of Student Debt on the Daily Lives of Older Americans.* https://file.asa.org/wp-content/uploads/2018/08/14141828/retirement-delayed-2017-1.pdf.

Berman, Jillian. 2018. "America's $1.5 Trillion Student-Loan Industry Is a 'Failed Social Experiment.'" MarketWatch, October 18, 2018. https://www.marketwatch.com/story/americas-15-trillion-student-debt-is-a-failed-social-experiment-2018-10-16?mod=article_inline.

Dickler, Jessica. 2017. "Student Loans Take a Mental Toll on Young People." CNBC, October 17, 2017. https://www.cnbc.com/2017/10/17/student-loans-take-a-mental-toll-on-young-people.html.

Health, Education, Labor, and Pensions (HELP) Committee. 2012. "For-Profit Higher Education: The Failure to Safeguard the Federal Investment and Ensure Student Success." U.S. Senate, July 30, 2012. https://www.help.senate.gov/imo/media/for_profit_report/PartI-PartIII-SelectedAppendixes.pdf.

Hembree, Diana. 2018. "New Report Finds Student Debt Burden Has 'Disastrous Domino Effect' on Millions of Americans." *Forbes,* November 1, 2018. https://www.forbes.com/sites/dianahembree/2018/11/01/new-report-finds-student-debt-burden-has-disastrous-domino-effect-on-millions-of-americans/#3953c90c12d1.

Hsu, Hua. 2019. "Student Debt Is Transforming the American Family." *New Yorker,* September 2, 2019. https://www.newyorker.com/magazine/2019/09/09/student-debt-is-transforming-the-american-family.

Insler, Shannon. 2017. "The Mental Toll of Student Debt: What Our Survey Shows." Student Loan Hero, September 7, 2017. https://studentloanhero.com/featured/psychological-effects-of-debt-survey-results/.

Keshner, Andrew. 2018. "How Student-Loan Debt Affects the Rest of Your Life (It's Not Pretty)." MarketWatch, November 20, 2018. https://www.marketwatch.com/story/what-student-debt-does-to-people-its-not-pretty-2018-11-14.

Looney, Adam, David Wessel, and Kadija Yilla. 2020. "Who Owes All That Student Debt? And Who'd Benefit if It Were Forgiven?" Brookings Institution, January 28, 2020. https://www.brookings.edu/policy2020/votervital/who-owes-all-that-student-debt-and-whod-benefit-if-it-were-forgiven/.

MacLellan, Lila. 2019. "It's Time to Talk about the Mental Health Effects of Student Loan Debt." Quartz, October 28, 2019. https://qz.com/work/1732070/the-emotional-toll-of-student-loan-debt-at-work/.

Nadworny, Elissa. 2019. "These Are the People Struggling the Most to Pay Back Student Loans." NPR, July 9, 2019. https://www.npr.org/2019/07/09/738985632/these-are-the-people-struggling-the-most-to-pay-back-student-loans.

Nadworny, Elissa, and Clare Lombardo. 2019. "'I'm Drowning': Those Hit Hardest by Student Loan Debt Never Finished College." NPR, July 18, 2019. https://www.npr.org/2019/07/18/739451168/i-m-drowning-those-hit-hardest-by-student-loan-debt-never-finished-college.

Newsome, Kenneth. 2020. "Real Student Debt Stories." Student Debt Crisis, April 14, 2020. https://studentdebtcrisis.org/read-student-debt-stories/.

Valenti, Joe, Sarah Edelman, and Tobin Van Ostern. 2013. "Student-Loan Debt Has a Rippling Negative Effect on the Broader Economy." American Progress, April 10, 2013. https://www.americanprogress.org/issues/higher-education/news/2013/04/10/60173/student-loan-debt-has-a-rippling-negative-effect-on-the-broader-economy/.

Zaloom, Caitlin. 2019. *Indebted: How Families Make College Work at Any Cost.* Princeton, NJ: Princeton University Press.

Proposals for Student Loan Forgiveness

A combination of increasing college costs, growing reliance on borrowing, and stagnant wages for college graduates has caused student debt to rise to unprecedented levels in the United States. As of 2020, around 45 million Americans held an estimated $1.6 trillion in outstanding student loans. Much of this staggering total has accumulated since the 2008 financial crisis and recession. In fact, the amount of student debt outstanding has doubled since 2010 and quadrupled since 2004 (McHarris and Imani 2020). Many borrowers struggle to repay their student loans for decades, which reduces their financial security, shapes their life decisions, and causes emotional distress. Student debt also restricts consumer spending and places a damper on economic growth.

Many progressive lawmakers have promoted plans for student debt forgiveness as a way to stimulate the U.S. economy and level the playing field for a generation of college students. According to some estimates, canceling all outstanding federal student loans could boost U.S. gross national product (GNP) by $108 billion per year over ten years (Taylor 2020). To prevent another student debt crisis from arising in the future, some proposals combine debt forgiveness with programs to make public college tuition-free or debt-free. Critics of student loan forgiveness argue that across-the-board debt cancellation rewards borrowers—including students from wealthy families who attended expensive private colleges—for making fiscally irresponsible decisions. In addition, critics contend that it is unfair to force taxpayers to pick up the tab for doctors, lawyers, engineers, and other professionals who derive significant financial benefits from earning advanced degrees.

Student Debt Relief Measures

In general, student loans offer fewer options for cancellation than other types of consumer credit. They cannot be discharged in bankruptcy, for instance, and they are among the only kinds of loans payments allowed to be garnished from borrowers' Social Security income. The U.S. Department of Education does forgive student loans in case of the borrower's death or total permanent disability, however, as well as in some cases when a college closes, commits fraud, or fails to deliver promised educational experiences or outcomes. In addition, the federal government offers a few student loan forgiveness programs as incentives to encourage borrowers to fill low-paying public-sector jobs. The Public Service Loan Forgiveness Program and other federal debt-discharge plans have come under criticism, however, for having complex qualification requirements and rejecting up to 99 percent of applications for loan forgiveness.

Given the limited options available for discharging student debt, many borrowers find themselves saddled with payments for decades. The student debt burden disproportionately impacts women and students of color, who typically must borrow more money to afford college and tend to earn lower salaries once they enter the workforce. Eighty-five percent of black undergraduates take out student loans, for instance, compared to less than 70 percent of all undergraduates, and their average loan balance at graduation is 13 percent higher. Black students who earn bachelor's degrees are also five times more likely to default on their student loans than white degree recipients (Nilsen 2019). Although women earn 56 percent of college degrees, they account for nearly 67 percent of all outstanding student loan debt. "Instead of being an equalizer that helps close the wealth gap between the rich and the poor, higher education in the U.S. reproduces inequality," according to an editorial in *Al Jazeera*. "It increases the indebtedness of communities who already suffer from high levels of income insecurity and economic precarity. It reinforces the cycle of poverty and the paycheck-to-paycheck life many marginalized families are forced to live, even if they are better educated. Parents with college degrees who have high levels of debt are unlikely to be able to afford higher education for their own children" (McHarris and Imani 2020).

Since the 2008 financial crisis and $700 billion federal bailout of Wall Street banks and investment firms, progressive activists have championed student loan forgiveness as a means of improving the financial fortunes of ordinary Americans. Beginning with Senator Bernie Sanders (I-VT) during his 2016 presidential campaign, several Democratic candidates have issued proposals for canceling student debt for some or all borrowers. Sanders's broad higher education proposal included forgiving all federal student loans and making public college free. He planned to pay for these programs by imposing a tax on stock trades. In her 2020 presidential campaign, Senator Elizabeth Warren (D-MA) promised to forgive up to $50,000 in student debt for borrowers making less than $100,000 in annual income. Her debt-relief plan gradually phased out for borrowers with incomes over $100,000, with those making over $250,000 annually receiving no benefits. Warren claimed that her plan would eliminate student debt for 75 percent of American borrowers. She planned to impose a wealth tax on the top 0.1 percent of households to pay for her plan, which she promised to implement on the first day of her presidency by executive order. Former vice president Joe Biden, in contrast, proposed expanding and improving the Public Service Loan Forgiveness Program and enrolling other borrowers in a simplified income-related payment plan that would forgive any unpaid balance after 20 years.

Some individuals and groups developed their own programs to help people who are struggling to pay off student loans. Rolling Jubilee, a group affiliated with the Occupy movement, uses money from charitable donations to purchase debt from banks for pennies on the dollar. The group has abolished $13 million in student debt and liberated 9,400 borrowers from student loan payments. In 2019, billionaire businessman Robert F. Smith announced his intention to pay off the entire $40 million student loan balance for the graduating class at historically black Morehouse College. Sociologists plan to observe the students to see whether the unexpected windfall alters their life decisions and career paths. Student loan cancellation also became the grand prize on a game show, *Paid Off with Michael Torpey,* that aired on TruTV. Each episode featured three recent college graduates competing in a trivia contest to win an amount equal to their education debt. "I want you to be pissed off that the show has to exist and that we're leaving students out in the cold," Torpey said of the satirical premise (Hsu 2019).

In March 2020, Congress debated several proposals for student debt for-giveness as part of economic relief measures to help the American people during the COVID-19 pandemic. Senate Democrats proposed immediately forgiving $10,000 in federal student loans for all borrowers. Supporters of the plan asserted that it would provide valuable assistance to low-income borrowers. They pointed out that the borrowers most likely to default on student loans held relatively low median balances of around $9,000, so the measure would eliminate their entire debt obligation. "By setting the number at $10,000, we are alleviating borrowers who are most in need," a congressional aide explained (Murakami 2020). House Democrats intro-duced a more expansive bill, the Student Debt Emergency Relief Act, that proposed canceling $30,000 in student loans for all borrowers. In addition, the legislation called on the Department of Education to freeze payments on any remaining balances until the pandemic ended and the economy returned to normal. Proponents of this plan argued that it would provide greater assistance to medical workers fighting on the front lines against the virus, many of whom accumulated large student debts to finance graduate degrees. As it turned out, however, student debt forgiveness did not appear in the first major relief legislation to address the COVID-19 pandemic. While the CARES Act froze payments and interest accrual on federal stu-dent loans, it did not apply to the $124 billion in outstanding private edu-cation loans, which were still subject to debt-collection activities by lenders (McHarris and Imani 2020).

Objections to Student Debt Forgiveness

One of the main criticisms leveled at student loan forgiveness programs is that, like many other forms of education funding, they tend to benefit middle- and upper-income students more than low-income students. Afflu-ent students are more likely to attend college, to choose expensive private institutions, and to pursue graduate and professional degrees. They are also less likely to qualify for need-based financial aid to reduce their tuition costs. As a result, wealthier students often account for larger student loan balances, although they are less likely to struggle with repayment. A Brook-ings Institution analysis of Warren's student loan forgiveness plan suggested that the top 40 percent of households would receive two-thirds of the ben-efits, while the bottom 60 percent of households would receive one-third. Only 4 percent of the benefits would accrue to borrowers in the lowest 20 percent income bracket (Looney 2019). "What we have in place and we need to improve is a system that says, 'If you cannot afford your loan payments, we will forgive them,'" said Urban Institute scholar Sandra Baum.

"Whether we should also have a program that says, 'Let's also forgive the loan payments even if you can afford them' is another question" (Looney, Wessel, and Yilla 2020).

While some proponents of student loan forgiveness prefer a targeted approach that extends relief mainly to low-income borrowers or people of color, they acknowledge that offering debt cancellation only to certain groups might be complicated and potentially illegal. In addition, supporters note that many borrowers who earn relatively high incomes may face family or medical issues that make it difficult for them to repay student loans. "The complaints about cancellation being regressive doesn't acknowledge there are very big differences in terms of income and wealth," said analyst Ashley Harrington of the Center for Responsible Lending. "I get a little frustrated because the argument doesn't acknowledge that making an income of $80,000 goes a lot further for one person than another" (Murakami 2020). Some advocates sought to prioritize debt cancellation for students victimized by for-profit college scams. "We'd like to see 100 percent forgiveness of those ripped off by for-profits and bad-actor, high-priced colleges with unconscionably high dropout rates," said Michael Dannenberg of Education Reform Now (Murakami 2020).

Some critics questioned the potential economic impact of student debt forgiveness, arguing that the benefits depended partly on the mechanism used to pay for the program. In addition to the $1.6 trillion in outstanding loans to be discharged, eliminating all student debt stood to cost the federal government $85 billion in lost principal, interest, and fees (Friedman 2020). Critics suggested that imposing new taxes on wealthy Americans or the financial services industry might blunt the expected stimulus effects of student loan relief, such as increased consumer spending, higher rates of homeownership, and small business formation. Some economists wondered whether forgiving mortgage loans or credit card debt might produce a more desirable economic impact, while others contemplated whether different funding methods would work better than raising taxes.

Finally, some critics contend that canceling outstanding student debt obligations amounts to an unfair or immoral use of taxpayer funds. People who worked hard for years to pay back their own student loans ask why current borrowers should not be expected to do the same. People who saved money for college to avoid student loans ask why they should miss out on the financial benefits. People who plan to take out student loans in the future ask whether their debts will eventually be forgiven. Other observers wonder if the expectation of student loan forgiveness will encourage tomorrow's students to borrow even more money for college, fueling further tuition increases and creating a new student debt crisis. "Loan forgiveness doubles down on the failed federal policies that led to the $1.6 trillion student loan crisis," wrote Heritage Foundation analyst Mary Clare Amselem. "Federal student loans offer colleges and universities excessive funds that enable them to raise their tuition without fear of losing customers. Instead, Americans should be holding colleges and universities accountable by tightening the purse strings coming from Washington" (Amselem 2019).

Further Reading

Amselem, Mary Clare. 2019. "No, Your Student Loans Should Not Be Forgiven." Heritage Foundation, July 1, 2019. https://www.heritage.org/education/commentary/no-your-student-loans-should-not-be-forgiven.

Friedman, Zack. 2020. "This Is What Happens if $1.6 Trillion of Student Loans Are Forgiven." *Forbes,* February 2, 2020. https://www.forbes.com/sites/zack-friedman/2020/02/02/student-loans-bernie-sanders-elizabeth-warren/#2f07e33035e1.

Hsu, Hua. 2019. "Student Debt Is Transforming the American Family." *New Yorker,* September 2, 2019. https://www.newyorker.com/magazine/2019/09/09/student-debt-is-transforming-the-american-family.

Looney, Adam. 2019. "How Progressive Is Senator Elizabeth Warren's Loan Forgiveness Proposal?" Brookings, April 24, 2019. https://www.brookings.edu/blog/up-front/2019/04/24/how-progressive-is-senator-elizabeth-warrens-loan-forgiveness-proposal/.

Looney, Adam, David Wessel, and Kadija Yilla. 2020. "Who Owes All That Student Debt? And Who'd Benefit if It Were Forgiven?" Brookings, January 28, 2020. https://www.brookings.edu/policy2020/votervital/who-owes-all-that-student-debt-and-whod-benefit-if-it-were-forgiven/.

McHarris, Philip V., and Zellie Imani. 2020. "It Is Time to Cancel Student Debt and Make Higher Education Free." *Al Jazeera,* April 26, 2020. https://www.aljazeera.com/indepth/opinion/time-cancel-student-debt-higher-education-free-200425104050766.html.

Murakami, Kery. 2020. "Is Canceling Student Debt the Right Approach?" *Inside Higher Ed,* April 1, 2020. https://www.insidehighered.com/news/2020/04/01/progressives-were-divided-over-widespread-cancellation-student-debt-stimulus.

Nilsen, Emma. 2019. "Progressives Want to Go Further Than Tuition-Free College—Here's Their Proposal to Make It Debt-Free." Vox, March 7, 2019. https://www.vox.com/2019/3/7/18252270/progressives-tuition-debt-free-college-schatz-pocan.

Taylor, Astra. 2020. "Cancelling Student Debt Was Always the Right Thing to Do. Now It's Imperative." *Guardian,* April 7, 2020. https://www.theguardian.com/commentisfree/2020/apr/07/cancel-student-debt-coronavirus.

CHAPTER FOUR

Profiles

This chapter provides illuminating biographical profiles of important figures in the development and implementation of U.S. higher education policy, including university administrator F. King Alexander, Secretary of Education Betsy DeVos, and former student loan ombudsman Seth Frotman. It also examines leading voices in the debate over college affordability and student debt, such as economist Bryan Caplan, consumer advocate Alan Collinge, and Democratic senator and presidential candidate Elizabeth Warren.

F. King Alexander (1963–)

University administrator and advocate of public funding for higher education

Fieldon King Alexander was born in October 1963 in Louisville, Kentucky. He was the second of four sons born to Ruth Hammack Alexander and Kern Alexander, who both served as college professors and higher education administrators. "People hand down businesses," he explained. "This is our family business" (Holt 2015). Kern Alexander worked for the U.S. Department of Education during the Lyndon B. Johnson administration, taught at the University of Florida and several other institutions, and served as president of Western Kentucky University and Murray State University. Ruth Alexander taught physical education and exercise science at several universities, including the University of Florida. She helped establish a women's intercollegiate athletics program at the school and testified before Congress in support of Title IX of the Higher Education Act, which required schools to provide equal educational and athletic opportunities for women.

King Alexander grew up in Gainesville, Florida. He earned a bachelor's degree in political science from St. Lawrence University in New York, where he played on the men's basketball team. Alexander went on to earn a master's degree in educational studies and comparative education policy from the University of Oxford in England, followed by a Ph.D. in higher education administration from the University of Wisconsin at Madison. His thesis examined the impact of 1972 amendments to the Higher Education Act that gave federal financial aid funds directly to students—in the form of Pell Grants and subsidized student loans—rather than channeling the money through states and public institutions. Alexander noted that this change allowed state and federal aid to flow to elite private colleges and for-profit institutions of dubious educational value, as well as to public community colleges and flagship state universities. Rather than increasing college access and affordability for low-income students as proponents claimed, he predicted that the direct-aid model would lead to reductions in state support for public institutions and higher tuition rates for students.

After receiving his doctorate, Alexander taught at the University of Illinois for several years. His academic interests focused on higher education funding and equity. In 2001, he came to national attention when his article "The Silent Crisis," which revealed a $20,000 average salary gap between professors at private and public universities, appeared in the *Economist*. A short time later, Alexander succeeded his father as president of Murray State University in Kentucky. In 2006, he left Murray State to become president of California State University-Long Beach. During his tenure, he oversaw an increase in enrollment as well as construction of a $70 million student recreation center and a $110 million science building. He was also twice selected as president of the year among the 23 public institutions in California's state university system.

In 2013, Alexander took over as chancellor of Louisiana State University (LSU) and president of the LSU system, which included four academic campuses and graduate schools in business, law, medicine, dentistry, and veterinary science. His appointment to head LSU aroused some controversy, with critics questioning whether he had the necessary academic and administrative credentials to oversee the operations of a major research institution. In addition, some insiders opposed the firing of Alexander's predecessor, John V. Lombardi, which allegedly took place at the behest of Louisiana governor Bobby Jindal. Leaders of the LSU faculty senate registered a vote of no confidence against the LSU board of supervisors as a protest over how they had conducted the search for a new president. Alexander defended his record, however, and joined a long history of LSU leaders that began with Union Army General William T. Sherman in 1859.

Alexander took the reins at LSU at a time when Jindal and the state legislature had proposed drastic cuts in appropriations for higher education in response to budget constraints brought on by an economic recession. Alexander strenuously resisted the proposed 80 percent cut in state funding, pointing out that Louisiana had already decreased per-pupil funding by 43 percent since 2008. When his efforts to sway key legislators failed, Alexander warned that the proposed level of state disinvestment might force LSU to declare "financial exigency"—the equivalent of academic bankruptcy. "It changed everything—those two words," recalled Bob Mann, a professor in LSU's school of communications (Holt 2015). Alexander's declaration garnered national media attention, caused a stir in Wall Street financial markets, and rallied Louisiana residents in support of their flagship state university. In the end, Jindal and the legislature restored state funding for higher education and found other ways to balance the budget.

For Alexander, the fight against the proposed budget cuts formed part of his larger argument in support of affordable, accessible public higher education. Noting that states spent about half as much on higher education in 2015 as they had 35 years earlier, he called upon policymakers to make federal education funding contingent upon states dedicating a certain percentage of tax revenues to public colleges and universities. Without this type of incentive, Alexander argued, states would slash higher education spending whenever they faced budget pressures, forcing public institutions to make up the difference by raising tuition. "As states backed out of their previous funding commitments, colleges and universities were forced to charge more just to cover basic costs and maintain competitiveness," he explained. "Studies have shown that more than 80 percent of public higher education tuition increases during the past two decades were directly related to state disinvestment" (Alexander 2016). As a result, low-income students struggled to afford to attend LSU, despite massive increases in federal spending on higher education grants, loans, and tax credits.

Alexander argued that making college affordable required the federal government to force states to contribute their fair share of higher education funding. This idea factored into the proposals for debt-free public college put forth by several Democratic presidential candidates, including senators Bernie Sanders and Elizabeth Warren. "If states continue on their current funding trajectory, the costs associated with any discussion about offering a free college education would be astronomical for the federal government," Alexander stated. "That's why the federal-state partnership is so important. This partnership will ensure that quality and affordable public college and university options remain available for generations to come by rewarding states that maintain their investment responsibilities to public higher education" (Alexander 2016).

Alexander also campaigned for greater transparency in higher education to promote institutional accountability and to ensure that students and families had all the information they needed to make good college decisions. He pointed out that while public universities had to report financial data to the government, private colleges and for-profit schools were largely exempt from reporting requirements, even though they received taxpayer funding through the direct-aid model. Alexander argued that full disclosure by all institutions would put public and private schools on the same plane and help rebuild public trust in the value of higher education. "Greater transparency can only help reduce the growing public perception that higher education no longer provides the social and economic returns that it once did—and it will help students separate high-quality institutions from the increasingly prevalent diploma mills," he wrote. "Increased accountability reassures the public that checks and balances are in place to ensure taxpayer dollars are being used efficiently and effectively" (Alexander 2018).

In 2019, Alexander announced his intention to leave LSU to assume the presidency at Oregon State University (OSU). He expressed appreciation for his time in Baton Rouge. "It's been a privilege to be part of such an important and iconic university system," he said. "I'm proud of what we've collectively accomplished, including setting records for enrollment in size, diversity, and academic achievement" (Gremillion and Jackson 2019). At the same time, Alexander noted that Oregon supported its public universities with higher annual funding than Louisiana. In fact, OSU anticipated a 12.3 percent increase in state funding, whereas Alexander predicted another political battle just to maintain state appropriations for LSU at their current level. "It'll be another dog fight," he stated. "We're not keeping up with the nation" (Ballard and Sentell 2019). In his personal life, Alexander is the father to two children. After losing his first wife, Elizabeth Williams Alexander, to breast cancer in 2000, he married his second wife, Shenette Campbell Alexander, in 2006.

Further Reading

Addo, Koran. 2013. "Alexander Defends Record." *The Advocate*, March 23, 2013. https://www.theadvocate.com/baton_rouge/news/education/article_1d78991f-3886-5a9c-988d-c96f78cbf8dd.html.

Alexander, F. King. 2016. "LSU President: If We Want Public Colleges to Be Affordable, a Federal-State Partnership Is Key." *Washington Post*, August 10,

2016. https://www.washingtonpost.com/news/grade-point/wp/2016/08/10/lsu-president-if-we-want-public-colleges-to-be-affordable-a-federal-state-partnership-is-key/.

Alexander, F. King. 2018. "Opinion: Is U.S. Higher Education Headed for 'Wild West' Tumult?" *Hechinger Report,* July 9, 2018. https://hechingerreport.org/opinion-is-us-higher-education-headed-for-wild-west-tumult/.

Ballard, Mark, and Will Sentell. 2019. "Answering Questions about F. King Alexander." *The Advocate,* December 13, 2019. https://www.theadvocate.com/baton_rouge/news/education/article_7ad8e13e-1dd3-11ea-8d7e-9765e3c5f5be.html.

Gremillion, Nick, and Donovan Jackson. 2019. "LSU President F. King Alexander Will Leave for Oregon State University." KSLA News, December 13, 2019. https://www.ksla.com/2019/12/13/lsu-president-f-king-alexander-will-leave-oregon-state-university/.

Holt, Alexander. 2015. "How One University President Is Trying to Save Public Higher Ed." *Atlantic,* September 23, 2015. https://www.theatlantic.com/education/archive/2015/09/lsu-debt-free-college/406555/.

Kelderman, Eric. 2019. "After Taking Heat in Louisiana, a President Moves to a More Moderate Climate." *Chronicle of Higher Education,* December 13, 2019. https://www.chronicle.com/article/After-Taking-Heat-in/247720.

Bryan Caplan (1971–)

Economist who proposed eliminating government subsidies for higher education

Bryan Douglas Caplan was born on April 8, 1971, in Northridge, California. He first developed an interest in libertarian ideas when a friend introduced him to Ayn Rand's *Atlas Shrugged* at Granada Hills High School. He soon began reading the works of prominent philosophers and questioning the economic benefits of policies that most people took for granted, such as minimum wages and immigration restrictions. Caplan earned a bachelor's degree in economics from the University of California at Berkeley in 1993, followed by a Ph.D. in economics from Princeton University in 1997.

After completing his education, Caplan joined the faculty at George Mason University (GMU). The school's namesake, the prominent Virginia planter and politician George Mason (1725-1792), helped draft the U.S. Constitution and fought to add the Bill of Rights to protect individual liberties. Caplan launched his career as an assistant professor of economics in 1997, became an associate professor in 2003, and received tenure as a full professor in 2010. "I have a dream job for life," he wrote. "GMU essentially pays me to do whatever I want, and I never have to retire" (Caplan 2018b). Caplan also served as a research fellow at GMU's Mercatus Center, a think tank devoted to free-market ideas, and as an adjunct scholar at the Cato Institute, a libertarian think tank focused on personal freedom and limited government.

Throughout his career, Caplan established a reputation as a "contrarian" economist who challenged conventional wisdom on many sociopolitical topics. He published hundreds of articles in academic journals and popular magazines, provided interviews and commentary for newspapers and news programs, appeared on the *Freakonomics* radio show and podcast, and contributed blog posts to EconLog. Caplan also expounded upon some of his economic theories in book form. In *The Myth of the Rational Voter: Why Democracies Choose Bad Policies* (2007), Caplan argued that voters made irrational choices based on systematically biased beliefs and fundamental misunderstandings about economic principles. He claimed that these choices undermined the functioning of democratic governments.

Caplan's next book, *Selfish Reasons to Have More Kids: Why Being a Great Parent Is Less Work and More Fun Than You Think* (2011), postulated that most people tended to overestimate the time, expense, and effort required to raise children, leading to unfounded fears about procreation and shrinking family sizes. Caplan argued that nature (genetics) played a more significant role than nurture (parenting) in determining whether children became successful, so he encouraged parents to take a more relaxed, positive approach to child-rearing and to have more children. The book generated a great deal of public discussion and media attention, as well as an invitation for Caplan to debate law professor Amy Chua, who espoused a strict, perfectionist "Tiger Mother" approach to parenting. Caplan also published *Open Borders: The Science and Ethics of Immigration* (2019), a graphic nonfiction book illustrated by Zach Weinersmith. It explored the controversy surrounding immigration and offered economic arguments in favor of eliminating restrictions, opening international borders, and allowing free global migration.

In 2018, Caplan published *The Case against Education: Why the Education System Is a Waste of Time and Money*. This influential book questioned the assumption that higher educational attainment for all citizens produced societal benefits and economic growth. This idea, which took root in the United States during the twentieth century, led to enormous government investment in education. It also convinced generations of Americans to pursue college degrees as a means of achieving prosperity, upward mobility, and personal fulfillment. Beginning in the 1980s, however, college tuition costs skyrocketed, causing more people to question the value of higher education. Caplan weighed into this debate by claiming that modern higher education did little to increase human capital by enhancing students' skills or preparing them to enter the workforce. "I'm not saying that college teaches *zero* real-world skills. My claim, rather, is that at least half of what colleges teach is not useful in the real world," he wrote. "If you actually measure learning, students usually learn little, quickly forget most of what they learn, and fail to apply what they still know even when their education is actually relevant" (Caplan 2018b).

Caplan asserted that a college degree mainly signaled to employers that an individual possessed attributes that predicted successful job performance. "Completing a degree—even a useless degree—signals to employers that you're smart, hard-working, and conformist," he stated. "Most people never finish college. If you do finish, you show the labor market that you've got the right stuff—and many doors open" (Caplan 2018b). Caplan estimated that job signaling accounted for more than half, and perhaps as much as 80 percent, of the financial rewards individuals obtained by earning a college degree. To prove his point, he noted that anyone who wanted an Ivy League education could get one for free by simply showing up at Princeton, Yale, or Harvard and attending classes. "No one will stop you. Professors will be flattered by your attendance," he said. "At the end of four years, you'll have a great education but no diploma" (Caplan 2018b). The student would not qualify for a high-paying job that required a bachelor's degree, however, even after completing all of the required coursework.

If higher education primarily provided job signaling rather than social and economic benefits, according to Caplan, then the massive government investments aimed at increasing college access and affordability went to waste. He pointed out that taxpayers spent an estimated $350 billion per year to subsidize higher education in the form of grants, loans, and tax benefits. Although these subsidies enabled more students to go to college, Caplan claimed that they also reduced the value of higher education to college graduates, because employers responded to the increase in qualified candidates by raising the credentials required in the job market. "Government subsidies are counter-productive," he explained. "When education gets cheaper, you just have to jump through more hoops to convince employers that you're in the top third of the distribution. Subsidizing college so we can all get better jobs is like urging us to stand up at a concert so we can all see better" (Caplan 2019a).

In direct opposition to proposals for tuition-free public college, Caplan recommended eliminating government funding for higher education and transitioning to a free-market system. Some critics charged that this approach would further increase college costs so that only students from wealthy families could access quality higher education. "What Caplan really should worry about is educational inequality," Joshua Kim wrote in a review for *Inside Higher Ed.* "Further cuts in public funding for higher education, as Caplan advocates for, will only increase the divide between educational haves and have-nots" (Kim 2018). In response, Caplan asserted that a free-market education system would be fairer to American taxpayers. "Suppose your parents had the money to pay for your college, but refused to do so," he wrote. "Would it be *fair* to legally force them to cough up the money? Probably not: You're an adult and it's their money. I say we should extend taxpayers the same courtesy. If your parents don't owe you an education, neither do millions of total strangers" (Caplan 2019a). Rather than incurring huge amounts of debt to pay for college, Caplan suggested that many students would be better off learning practical skills through vocational education. His book recommended replacing traditional liberal arts-oriented education with career-based training programs.

On his website, Caplan described himself as "an openly nerdy man who loves role-playing games and graphic novels" (Caplan 2019b). He married his college sweetheart, Corina Mateescu, in 1994. They raised four children—twin sons Aidan and Tristan, son Simon, and daughter Valeria—in Oakton, Virginia. As an economist, Caplan remained committed to promoting libertarian ideas and policies. "Trying to make the world a freer place has turned out to be the best job in the world," he noted. "I continue to look forward to a lifetime of thinking about the Big Questions and going wherever my curiosity takes me" (Caplan 2010).

Further Reading

Caplan, Bryan. 2010. "An Intellectual Autobiography." In Block, Walter, ed., *I Chose Liberty: Autobiographies of Contemporary Libertarians,* pp. 73-82. Auburn, AL: Ludwig von Mises Institute. https://cdn.mises.org/I%20Chose%20Liberty%20Autobiographies%20of%20Contemporary%20Libertarians_2.pdf.

Caplan, Bryan. 2018a. *The Case against Education: Why the Education System Is a Waste of Time and Money.* Princeton, NJ: Princeton University Press.

Caplan, Bryan. 2018b. "The World Might Be Better Off without College for Everyone." *Atlantic,* January/February 2018. https://www.theatlantic.com/magazine/archive/2018/01/whats-college-good-for/546590/.

Caplan, Bryan. 2019a. "Higher Education: Why Government Should Cut the Cord." Opening Statement, The Pearlstein-Caplan Debate: Should We Stop Funding Higher Education? http://econfaculty.gmu.edu/bcaplan/pearlsteindebate.htm.

Caplan, Bryan. 2019b. "Site Homepage." BCaplan.com, 2019. http://bcaplan.com/index.html.

Kim, Joshua. 2018. "The Case against *The Case against Education*." *Inside Higher Ed,* October 18, 2018. https://www.insidehighered.com/blogs/technology-and-learning/case-against-case-against-education.

Alan Collinge (1970–)

Consumer protection advocate and founder of Student Loan Justice

Alan Michael Collinge was born on March 3, 1970. Growing up in Tacoma, Washington, he shared the modest aspirations of his peers, which included a college education, a good job, and a comfortable life with a home and family. As a means of achieving those goals, Collinge attended the University of Southern California, where he completed three degrees in aerospace engineering. To finance his education in an era of rapidly rising college costs, he took out $38,000 in student loans. By the time he graduated in 1998, compounded interest and fees had increased his total student debt to nearly $50,000.

Like many young people in the late 1980s and 1990s, Collinge viewed a college education as a necessary step toward achieving the middle-class lifestyle he wanted, and he used student loans as a tool to help him reach his dreams. The U.S. government established federally guaranteed student loans through the Higher Education Act of 1965 to increase access to college for students of limited means. As college costs increased at more than twice the rate of inflation, however, more and more students were forced to borrow money to pay for their educations. By 2018, 45 million Americans owed more than $1.5 trillion in student loan debt—making it the second-highest source of consumer debt in the United States, behind only home mortgages and ahead of outstanding credit card balances and auto loans (Friedman 2019). For many college graduates, student loan debt created a financial burden that prevented them from taking vacations, buying homes, starting families, saving for retirement, or achieving other goals.

After finishing his degrees, Collinge worked as an aeronautical research scientist at the California Institute of Technology (Caltech). He consolidated his student loans through a program offered by Sallie Mae, which had started out as a government-sponsored entity but had recently changed to a private-sector, for-profit business enterprise. At $600 per month, Collinge's loan payments to Sallie Mae accounted for 20 percent of his starting salary, and the remainder barely covered his rent, utilities, food, car, and other necessities.

In 1999, Collinge encountered an unforeseen expense and came up short on a single student loan payment. "I called the lender and was assured that as long as I continued to make my regularly scheduled payments, all would be well, with the exception of a one-time late fee on the account," he recalled (Collinge 2009, viii). Six months later, however, Collinge realized that Sallie Mae had charged him a late fee every month, even though he had followed the lender's instructions and continued making his regular payments. Assuming the company had made a mistake, Collinge requested that Sallie Mae remove the fees, but the lender refused. As Collinge grew increasingly frustrated with Sallie Mae, he looked into refinancing his student loans with another company that offered better customer service— only to learn that federal regulations prohibited student borrowers from refinancing beyond a one-time initial consolidation.

By 2001, Collinge found that he could no longer meet his living expenses and make his student loan payments on his salary as an aeronautics researcher. He quit his job at Caltech in hopes of finding a higher-paying job in the defense industry. "Unfortunately, the events of September 11 put a chill on the economy, and instead of having a six-figure defense job, I was unemployed," Collinge remembered. "In retrospect, leaving Caltech without a job lined up was a big mistake, one that I will live with for the rest of my life" (Collinge 2009, viii).

Relegated to sleeping on friends' couches while he desperately looked for a job, Collinge contacted Sallie Mae to request a forbearance—a temporary pause on loan payments, during which interest and fees continued to accrue—due to economic hardship. To his shock, the lender denied his request and immediately put his loan in default. By this time, Collinge had made payments totaling around $25,000, and Sallie Mae stood to collect the remaining principal balance from the federal government, which guaranteed most student loans. Yet the company transferred Collinge's debt to a guarantor called EdFund, which in turn hired a collection agency called General Revenue Corporation that was a subsidiary of Sallie Mae.

Over the next few years, Collinge took a series of odd jobs, working 90 hours per week at minimum wage without time off "to somehow serve as a penance" for his financial mistakes (Collinge 2009, x). While he tried in vain to negotiate a repayment plan with Sallie Mae, EdFund, and even the U.S. Department of Education, Collinge watched his loan balance grow steadily by more than $1,000 per month until it eventually exceeded $100,000. "I found that I had no negotiation power whatsoever for my student loan debts," he recalled. "Bankruptcy does not eliminate them, statutes of limitations do not exist for them, and the standard consumer protections on other types of debts do not apply" (Collinge 2009, x). Meanwhile, Collinge endured a constant barrage of harassment, intimidation, and humiliation from collection agencies. The experience destroyed his credit record, making it impossible for him to get the security clearance needed to work as an aerospace engineer, and took a toll on his mental and physical health. "It does affect your self-esteem," Collinge acknowledged. "There's a certain shame involved" (Schorn 2006).

In 2005, after learning more about the student debt crisis, Collinge launched a website called StudentLoanJustice.org "to try and force a political solution by connecting with the millions of people who shared my fate, exposing the individuals who had engineered—and profited tremendously from—this uniquely predatory system, and helping to spur Congress to fix the problem" (Collinge 2009, xii). He collected stories from hundreds of borrowers who struggled to repay their student debt, posted research showing how companies like Sallie Mae profited at the expense of college graduates, and called for legislation to restore consumer protections and end predatory lending practices in the student loan industry.

Collinge's cause soon began to attract media attention, and his organization received mention in such publications as *Fortune* magazine, the *New York Times,* the *Washington Post,* and the *Chronicle of Higher Education.* In 2006, the television news program *60 Minutes* interviewed Collinge and other StudentLoanJustice.org members for a segment on the student loan industry. This exposure led to other television and radio features, as well as inquiries from such well-known consumer advocates as Ralph Nader and Michael Moore. Collinge formed a grassroots political action committee, Student Loan Justice, which maintained its independence by only accepting donations from individuals, rather than corporations, institutions, or government agencies. Some of the group's 4,000 members worked with then-Senator Hillary Clinton (D-NY) and her staff to develop a legislative package called the Student Borrower Bill of Rights. In 2008, CNN/ *Money Magazine* selected Collinge as one of its "Financial Heroes" for his work on student loan reform.

In 2009, Collinge published an influential book based on his experiences, *The Student Loan Scam: The Most Oppressive Debt in U.S. History—and How We Can Fight Back.* He traced the history of the student loan industry, examined who benefitted from the elimination of consumer protections, and offered legislative solutions as well as advice for borrowers. The book also included numerous stories from ordinary citizens who had their lives and livelihoods ruined by mountains of student debt and unscrupulous collection practices. *Publishers Weekly* gave it a starred review, describing it as a "shocking exposé" and "whistle-blowing at its finest" ("Pick of the Week," 2008). Collinge's book remained relevant a decade after its publication, as the number of Americans in default on student loans reached 5 million in 2019, and proposals to solve the student debt crisis dominated political discussions.

Further Reading

Collinge, Alan Michael. 2009. *The Student Loan Scam: The Most Oppressive Debt in U.S. History—and How We Can Fight Back.* Boston: Beacon Press.

Hsu, Hua. 2019. "Student Debt Is Transforming the American Family." *New Yorker,* September 9, 2019. https://www.newyorker.com/magazine/2019/09/09/student-debt-is-transforming-the-american-family.

O'Shaugnessy, Lynn. "Hero: Alan Collinge." CNN/*Money*, December 12, 2008. https://money.cnn.com/galleries/2008/news/0812/gallery.heroes_zeros_2008/5.html.

"Pick of the Week Book Review: *The Student Loan Scam.*" *Publishers Weekly,* October 6, 2008. https://www.publishersweekly.com/978-0-8070-4229-8.

Schorn, Daniel. 2006. "Sallie Mae's Success Too Costly?" *60 Minutes,* CBS News, May 5, 2006. https://www.cbsnews.com/news/sallie-maes-success-too-costly/5/.

Randall Collins (1941–)

Sociologist who raised questions about the value of higher education

Randall Collins was born on July 29, 1941, in Knoxville, Tennessee. As the son of a career diplomat who served in the U.S. Department of State, Collins spent most of his childhood living in American embassies around the world, including Berlin and Moscow. Collins completed his last two years of high school at a prestigious New England preparatory academy, where he first recognized inequalities in the American system of education. Most of his classmates hailed from wealthy families, and the curriculum was designed to help them gain admission to elite Ivy League universities. "What I learned about education at that point in my life was that it was stratified, some schools were considered more elite, and it was mainly children of rich families who went there," Collins remembered. "But even if your family wasn't rich (my father never owned a house until he retired), if you could get into an elite school, its high status would rub off on you too" (Collins 2018).

Collins went on to attend Harvard University, earning a bachelor's degree in psychology in 1962. He then pursued graduate study in psychology at Stanford University, earning a master's degree in 1964. Upon entering the University of California at Berkeley, Collins changed his area of emphasis to sociology. During the turbulent 1960s, he became involved in campus protests against U.S. involvement in the Vietnam War and in favor of students' rights as part of the Free Speech movement. He also studied with such influential sociologists as Joseph Ben-David, Reinhard Bendix, Herbert Blumer, Erving

Goffman, Leo Löwenthal, and Philip Selznick. Collins earned a second master's degree in sociology from Berkeley and completed his Ph.D. in 1969.

During his college years, Collins became part of a group of young sociologists interested in social conflict theory. This school of thought characterized human society as a perpetual competition for power and limited resources, which created conflict and drove social change. Collins published his first book on the subject, *Conflict Sociology,* in 1975. His next book grew out of his doctoral dissertation, entitled *Education and Employment: Some Determinants of Requirements for Hiring in Various Types of Organizations,* which examined the tendency for employers to require higher and higher levels of educational qualifications for the same jobs over time. Collins described this phenomenon as "credential inflation" and claimed that it diminished the value of advanced degrees, forcing students to seek more and more education.

In 1979, Collins expanded upon these ideas in *The Credential Society: A Historical Sociology of Education and Stratification,* which generated controversy by challenging the American system of higher education. "Originally my book was considered scandalous by many people," Collins acknowledged. "When I presented the original manuscript to my first publisher (University of California Press), they refused to accept it, even though it was under contract. A new publisher, Academic Press, published it, but then they refused to allow a mass paperback publisher (Anchor Books) to buy the rights to it, and Academic Press refused to issue it in paperback. So the book became hard to buy; and people would write to me to ask for a copy" (Collins 2018). *The Credential Society* eventually came to be considered a classic in its field for accurately predicting some of the problems that faced higher education four decades later. In recognition of its continuing relevance, Columbia University Press reissued it in a "Legacy Edition" with new forewords in 2019.

During the 1980s and 1990s, Collins published several books examining the sociological foundations of large-scale geopolitical events, such as wars, ethnic conflicts, and the formation of nation-states. As part of this work, he famously predicted the fall of the Soviet Union many years before it happened in 1991. One of Collins's best-known books, *The Sociology of Philosophies: A Global Theory of Intellectual Change* (1998), analyzed major intellectual traditions from around the world through history and developed a collective theory of the creation of knowledge. In the early 2000s, Collins shifted his focus toward the sociology of everyday, individual, face-to-face encounters and relationships. *Interaction Ritual Chains* (2004) and *Violence: A Micro-Sociological Theory* (2008) explored the role of emotional energies and interaction rituals in group behavior and social action.

Collins served on the faculties of several institutions during his career—including the University of California, San Diego (1969-1977), the University of Virginia (1978-1982), and the University of California, Riverside (1985-1997)—before becoming the Dorothy Swaine Thomas Professor of Sociology Emeritus at the University of Pennsylvania. Consistent with his criticism of educational credential inflation, he focused his work in academia on scholarly research rather than teaching. "It is rather pleasant to work in a high-level research university, so my only objection to working there was my moral objection to living off an institution that operates on false promises," he explained. "But it is interesting to work around intellectually creative colleagues and thoughtful students—especially if they are more interested in intellectual discoveries than in getting credentials" (Collins 2018).

Collins served as the president of the American Sociological Association (2010-2011) and twice received that organization's Distinguished Scholarship Award for his work. "Randall Collins is arguably one of the world's leading social theorists and probably the most prominent American sociologist," Siniša Malešević and Steven Loyal wrote in their introduction to a special issue of *Thesis Eleven* dedicated to Collins. "He has made an enormous contribution to sociological theory, the study of state formation, power, violence, sociology of the family, social stratification, sociology of emotions, historical and political sociology, the sociology of education, and the sociology of intellectuals" (Malešević and Loyal 2019).

Further Reading

Collins, Randall. 2018. "Educational Credential Inflation: An Interview with Randall Collins." The Sociological Eye (blog), July 19, 2018. http://sociological-eye.blogspot.com/2018/07/educational-credential-inflation.html.

Collins, Randall. 2019. *The Credential Society: A Historical Sociology of Education and Stratification*. Legacy Edition. New York: Columbia University Press.

Malešević, Siniša, and Steven Loyal. 2019. "Introduction to Special Issue: The Sociology of Randall Collins." *Thesis Eleven* 154(1), October 2019. https://doi.org/10.1177/0725513619874435.

"Randall Collins (1964)." 2019. University of California Berkeley, Department of Sociology. https://sociology.berkeley.edu/randall-collins-1964.

Turner, Jonathan. 2010. "Randall Collins: A Smart and Influential Theorist." American Sociological Association. https://www.asanet.org/randall-collins.

Betsy DeVos (1958–)

Private school advocate and secretary of education in the Trump Administration

Betsy DeVos was born Elizabeth Prince on January 8, 1958, in Grand Rapids, Michigan. She was the oldest of four children born to Elsa and Edgar Prince, who raised their family in nearby Holland, a prosperous town tucked along the Lake Michigan shoreline. Her mother worked as a public school teacher, while her father was a business entrepreneur who became wealthy after one of his inventions—lighted vanity mirrors on automobile sun visors—caught on with car manufacturers around the world. Many accounts of DeVos's childhood indicate that she spent her early years surrounded by opulence and wealth, but she later insisted that "it was not until I was in college that the business really became successful" (Nordlinger 2018).

DeVos attended Holland Christian High School, a private religious school. After graduating, she enrolled at Calvin College (now Calvin University), a private Christian liberal arts school in Grand Rapids. DeVos made her first foray into politics during her college years, volunteering for a variety of Republican campaigns and causes. In 1979, she earned a bachelor's degree in business economics from Calvin. That same year, she married Richard "Dick" DeVos, a billionaire heir to the Amway Corporation fortune. They settled in the Grand Rapids area, where they raised four children.

Over the next several decades, Betsy and Dick DeVos became perhaps the best-known couple in western Michigan, if not the entire state. Their high public profile stemmed from several factors. For one, they emerged as important figures in the Republican Party at both the state and national levels. Betsy DeVos represented Michigan on the Republican National Committee (RNC), the chief policymaking and fundraising arm of the Republican Party, from 1992 to 1997. In addition, she served as chair of the Michigan Republican Party from 1996 to 2000 and again from 2003 to 2005. Her husband Dick, meanwhile, was the Republican nominee for Michigan governor in 2006, but he lost to Democratic incumbent Jennifer Granholm. The couple also became known as major donors to conservative Christian organizations and Republican politicians.

Another factor contributing to DeVos's fame was the extent to which her family lent time and money to charitable and philanthropic causes in the Grand Rapids area. DeVos and her husband volunteered at and provided financial assistance to K-12 Christian schools around the city, and they funneled millions of dollars into various religious, community, and commercial enterprises around Grand Rapids. "The family's name and money are every-where," reported *Atlantic Magazine* in 2017. "There's the DeVos Perfor-mance Hall and the DeVos Place Convention Center anchoring downtown. Calvin College to the southeast boasts the DeVos Communica-tion Center, and Grand Rapids Christian High School (where the DeVos children went) has the DeVos Center for Arts and Worship. There's a DeVos Children's Hospital.... Even residents who say they oppose [DeVos's] poli-tics expressed a general understanding that the extended DeVos family has played a key role in revitalizing this city" (DeRuy 2017). Betsy DeVos also served on the boards of numerous national and local charitable and civic organizations, ranging from the Kennedy Center for the Performing Arts in Washington, D.C., to the Kendall College of Art and Design in down-town Grand Rapids.

Another key factor in raising the visibility of the DeVos name across Michigan was Betsy DeVos's emergence as one of the country's leading advocates for charter schools and "school choice," which allowed students to use "vouchers" (public funds) to pay tuition and enroll in private schools rather than attend local public schools. DeVos and other school choice sup-porters claimed that it gave valuable options to families of all income groups looking to secure a quality education for their children. Critics, however, contended that charter schools siphoned money away from public school systems that needed those funds. Detractors also asserted that allowing public funds to go to religious schools—many private K-12 schools have explicit religious affiliations—violated Constitutional guarantees of church-state separation. Finally, opponents of school choice emphasized that while federal law required public schools to accommodate all students, private schools did not have to accept students with disabilities or those of different religious faiths.

In 1993, DeVos and her fellow school choice activists celebrated the pas-sage of a Michigan law that permitted the opening of charter schools across the state. As charter schools sprouted up in many communities, though, DeVos did not rest. Instead, she became involved in efforts all across the country to expand school choice and privatize America's K-12 education system. DeVos's continued activism in education policy, combined with her family's deep ties to the Republican Party, ultimately led Donald Trump to nominate her to lead the U.S. Department of Education after his surprise presidential victory in November 2016.

Although school choice advocates applauded Trump's choice of DeVos as secretary of education, many public school teachers and administrators reacted with alarm. They pointed out that DeVos had been nominated to oversee the nation's public education system, even though neither she nor any of her children had ever worked at or attended a public school. They also emphasized that while some of the charter schools that DeVos had launched in Michigan performed at a high level, most of them posted lower academic scores than traditional public schools across the state. Critics charged that inadequate regulation of Michigan charter schools "has led to marginal and, in some cases, terrible schools in the state's poorest communities as part of a system dominated by for-profit operators. Charter-school growth has also weakened the finances and enrollment of traditional public-school districts" (Emma 2016).

Despite these criticisms, most political observers expected DeVos to win confirmation as the nation's 11th secretary of education fairly easily. During her January 2017 confirmation hearing before a U.S. Senate committee, however, she made several remarks that galvanized opposition to her nomination. DeVos's responses to a number of questions heightened concerns that she was unfamiliar with such fundamental aspects of the American education system as student testing practices, college financial aid and student loans, and the rights of students with disabilities. Critics also mocked DeVos's response to a question from Senator Chris Murphy of Connecticut, where a gunman had killed 20 children at Sandy Hook Elementary School in 2013, asking whether she thought guns "have any place in or around schools." DeVos said that decisions about arming teachers and other school staff should be left to local and state officials, then added that schools in places like Wyoming might need guns to protect students from "potential grizzlies" (Nelson 2017).

When DeVos's nomination came up for a final Senate vote, two Republicans—Lisa Murkowski (AK) and Susan Collins (ME)—joined all 48 Democrats in opposing her. The 50-50 tie in the Senate forced Vice President Mike Pence to cast a rare tie-breaking vote in order to seat her as the new head of the Department of Education. DeVos formally took the oath of office on February 7, 2017.

During her time as secretary of education, DeVos remained a lightning rod of controversy. Her supporters—primarily Republicans, religious conservatives, and supporters of school choice and free-market–based education reforms—praised her for rescinding education guidelines established by the Barack Obama administration that, in their view, trampled on the authority of state and local school systems. Her continued championing of school choice also won her warm praise from conservative religious organizations and likeminded education reformers. DeVos's defenders also alleged that her political opponents treated her unfairly. "Betsy DeVos is the unlikeliest villain you ever met," wrote conservative journalist Jay Nordlinger. "She is warm, polite, earnest, and generous. A wealthy woman, she has devoted her life to getting poor children a better shot at life" (Nord-linger 2018).

Critics, however, described her tenure as catastrophic on a number of fronts. They condemned her call to end federal funding for the Special Olympics (a proposal on which she quickly reversed course); accused her of dismantling Obama-era policies designed to protect the civil rights of LGBTQ students, minorities, and victims of campus sexual assault; and charged that her continued push for expansion of school choice and voucher programs around the country harmed traditional public schools.

DeVos's record on college student loans and for-profit colleges came under particularly intense scrutiny. During the mid-2010s, the Obama administration instituted a variety of reforms to clamp down on unscrupulous for-profit colleges that defrauded and victimized tens of thousands of students. It also introduced significant reforms to the nation's college financial aid and student loan programs to better protect student borrowers and reduce student debt. DeVos and other Trump administration officials, however, rescinded or rolled back most of these measures to protect college students from well-documented abuses. "The Trump team," wrote business journalist Jordan Weissmann, "has shown less concern for the plight of student borrowers than for the companies that want to make a buck off them" (Weissmann 2018).

Further Reading

DeRuy, Emily. 2017. "A Tale of Two Betsy DeVoses." *Atlantic,* March 8, 2017. https://www.theatlantic.com/education/archive/2017/03/a-tale-of-two-betsy-devoses/518952/.

Emma, Caitlin, Benjamin Wermund, and Kimberly Hefling. 2016. "DeVos' Michigan Schools Experiment Gets Poor Grades." *Politico,* December 9, 2016. https://www.politico.com/story/2016/12/betsy-devos-michigan-school-experiment-232399.

Leonard, Devin, and Shahien Nasiripour. 2019. "Trump Picked His Perfect Education Secretary in Betsy DeVos." *Bloomberg BusinessWeek,* July 17, 2019. https://www.bloomberg.com/news/features/2019-07-17/trump-picked-the-perfect-education-secretary-in-betsy-devos.

Nelson, Libby. 2017. "How Betsy DeVos Became Trump's Most Controversial Nominee." Vox, February 7, 2017. https://www.vox.com/policy-and-politics/2017/2/1/14475290/betsy-devos-confirmation-trump-resist.

Nordlinger, Jay. 2018. "Betsy DeVos and the Matter of Fairness." *National Review,* November 13, 2018. https://www.nationalreview.com/2018/11/betsy-devos-education-secretary-matter-of-fairness/.

Schneider, Jack, and Jennifer Berkshire. 2020. *A Wolf at the Schoolhouse Door: The Dismantling of Public Education and the Future of School.* New York: New Press.

Stahl, Jeremy. 2019. "This Is Still Happening: Betsy DeVos." Slate, October 30, 2019. https://slate.com/news-and-politics/2019/10/still-happening-trump-corruption-betsy-devos.html.

Weissmann, Jordan. 2018. "The Government's Student Loan Watchdog Quit in Disgust This Week. Here's What the Conflict Is Really About." Slate, August 29, 2018. https://slate.com/business/2018/08/cfpb-ombudsman-resigns-heres-what-seth-frotmans-letter-was-really-about.html.

Seth Frotman (1978?–)

Former student loan ombudsman for the Consumer Financial Protection Bureau

Seth Frotman earned a bachelor's degree in business administration from the University of Michigan in 2000. Four years later, he received a law degree from the University of Indiana, where he served as editor of the *Indiana Law Review.* After passing the bar in New Jersey, Frotman clerked in the U.S. Court of Appeals for the Third Circuit. He also worked on state-level consumer protection laws as a staff counsel for the New Jersey legislature. In 2007, he moved to Washington, D.C., to become deputy chief of staff and legislative director for U.S. Representative Patrick Murphy (D-PA).

In 2011, Frotman went to work for the newly established Consumer Financial Protection Bureau (CFPB). Congress created this federal agency through passage of the Dodd-Frank Wall Street Reform and Consumer Protection Act, which President Barack Obama signed into law in the wake of a global financial crisis that sent the U.S. economy spiraling into a severe recession. Critics blamed high-risk business practices by Wall Street banks and investment firms and demanded increased government regulation of the financial services industry. The CFPB worked to protect consumers from abusive practices by banks, mortgage companies, credit card companies, student loan servicers, and other powerful business interests. Senator Elizabeth Warren (D-MA), who oversaw creation of the CFPB, emphasized the importance of this mission. "You are all critical to cleaning up the abuses that have laid holy hell on American families," Frotman recalled her saying. "I expect all of you to do your job to the fullest, and when you do that, I will have your back" (Stewart 2019).

Frotman spent four years working in the CFPB's office of servicemember affairs as a senior advisor to Assistant Director Holly Petraeus. He received an award for excellence from the U.S. Secretary of Defense for helping to protect servicemembers, veterans, and military families from predatory lending practices. In 2014, Frotman served as an advisor to the Senate Committee on Health, Education, Labor, and Pensions (HELP) in its legislative efforts to develop new consumer protections for student loan borrowers. In 2015, Frotman shifted over to the CFPB's office for students and young consumers, where he assumed the positions of assistant director and student loan ombudsman. He thus took charge of investigating student loan complaints, recommending policy reforms to protect borrowers' interests, and cracking down on abusive practices by lenders, servicers, and debt collectors.

From its creation in 2011 through 2017, the CFPB student loan ombudsman's office reviewed more than 60,000 consumer complaints and returned more than $750 million to student borrowers it determined to have been deceived or treated unfairly (Turner 2018). Frotman oversaw a lawsuit against Navient (formerly Sallie Mae), a major student lender and servicer, that accused the company of misleading borrowers, processing payments incorrectly, failing to respond to complaints, and overcharging interest and fees. The ombudsman's office also launched investigations and enforcement actions against for-profit institutions of higher learning, such as Corinthian Colleges and ITT Technical Institute, that received large numbers of fraud complaints.

After President Donald Trump took office in 2017, his Republican administration took steps to reduce the CFPB's regulatory and enforcement powers. Frotman and others in the student loan ombudsman's office grew increasingly frustrated with actions they felt undermined their ability to protect student borrowers from misinformation, mistakes, and mismanagement by loan servicers. Mick Mulvaney, who became acting director of the CFPB in November 2017, was a vocal critic of the agency during his tenure in Congress and once referred to it as a "joke" (Turner 2018a). As director, he reorganized the student loan office and placed it within the CFPB's financial education area, thus shifting its emphasis from consumer protection to consumer information. Although Mulvaney downplayed the move as a "modest organizational chart change," consumer advocates claimed that it eliminated an important source of protection for student borrowers (Turner 2018).

The Trump administration also severed the relationship between the CFPB and the Department of Education, making it more difficult for Frotman's office to investigate complaints and enforce federal regulations. In August 2017, Secretary of Education Betsy DeVos announced that her department would no longer share student loan data with the CFPB, describing the agency as "overreaching and unaccountable" (Turner 2018). DeVos also moved to protect student loan servicers from state-level oversight, arguing that private contractors working for the federal government were immune from lawsuits brought by state attorneys general.

In August 2018, Frotman resigned from his position as CFPB student loan ombudsman. In a scathing letter addressed to Mulvaney, he asserted that the agency no longer represented the interests of ordinary Americans seeking to build better lives for their families. "You have used the bureau to serve the wishes of the most powerful financial companies in America," he wrote. "The damage you have done to the bureau betrays these families and sacrifices the financial futures of millions of Americans in communities across the country" (Associated Press 2018). Frotman's decision garnered praise from Petraeus, his former boss at CFPB. "Seth is a true public servant," she stated. "I think he's leaving for the purest of motives: He wants to help student borrowers" (Turner 2018). CFPB leaders refused to comment on Frotman's departure except to thank him for his service. Mulvaney's controversial tenure at CFPB ended in December 2018, when he accepted a position as acting chief of staff in the Trump White House.

Frotman's resignation received national news coverage and led to congressional hearings on the federal government's handling of the student debt crisis. After leaving the CFPB, Frotman gave lectures, wrote articles, testified before Congress, and advised state policymakers about the effects of student debt on individuals and the U.S. economy. Along with several other former CFPB regulators, he founded the Student Borrower Protection Center, a nonprofit organization dedicated to protecting the rights of borrowers, curbing abuses by the student loan industry, and promoting policy reforms to better serve future generations of students. "Student loan borrowers are being ripped off from the day they receive their first bill, to the day they pay off their loans," according to the SBPC website. "They struggle while billion-dollar companies profit by exploiting their financial distress" (Student Borrower Protection Center 2020).

Further Reading

Associated Press. 2018. "Top U.S. Student Loans Official Resigns over 'Open Hostility' from White House." *Guardian*, August 27, 2018. https://www.theguardian.com/us-news/2018/aug/27/seth-frotman-student-loan-ombudsman-resigns-white-house-hostility.

Frotman, Seth. 2017. "Staying on Track while Giving Back." Consumer Financial Protection Bureau, June 2017. https://files.consumerfinance.gov/f/documents/201706_cfpb_PSLF-midyear-report.pdf.

Frotman, Seth. 2019. "Testimony before the United States Congress House Finan-
    cial Services Committee." Student Borrower Protection Center, March 7,
    2019. https://financialservices.house.gov/uploadedfiles/hhrg-116-ba00-
    wstate-frotmans-20190307.pdf.
Stewart, Emily. 2019. "Elizabeth Warren Has Just One Plan." Vox, September 20,
    2019. https://www.vox.com/policy-and-politics/2019/9/20/20867899/
    elizabeth-warren-cfpb-founding-plans-obama-president.
Student Borrower Protection Center. 2020. "About Us." https://
    protectborrowers.org/about-us/.
Turner, Cory. 2018. "Student Loan Watchdog Quits, Says Trump Administration
    'Turned Its Back' on Borrowers." NPR, August 27, 2018. https://
    www.npr.org/2018/08/27/642199524/student-loan-watchdog-quits-
    blames-trump-administration.

Betsy Mayotte (1973?–)

*Borrowers' rights advocate and founder of the Institute of Student Loan
Advisors*

Betsy Mayotte was born and raised in Lowell, Massachusetts. In the
1990s, she attended Bentley University in Waltham, Massachusetts. By the
time she graduated with a bachelor's degree in business communication,
Mayotte had accumulated around $15,000 in student loan debt. The U.S.
government established federally guaranteed student loans through the
Higher Education Act of 1965 to increase access to college for students of
limited means. As college costs increased at more than twice the rate of
inflation, however, more and more students were forced to borrow money
to pay for their educations. By 2018, 45 million Americans owed more than
$1.5 trillion in student loan debt—making it the second-highest source of
consumer debt in the United States, behind only home mortgages and
ahead of outstanding credit card balances and auto loans.

Mayotte ended up finding work in the student loan industry as a compliance officer for American Student Assistance (ASA), a nonprofit organization based in Boston. ASA focused on providing guidance to people
seeking to secure or pay off education loans for college. Mayotte spent a
total of eighteen years at ASA, during which time she became well-versed
in virtually all aspects of college financial aid and student loan programs,
practices, and regulations. She also embraced the organization's advocacy
work on behalf of college students forced to take out loans in order to afford
to earn degrees. "I consider myself very lucky to have worked for an organization that focused so much on the borrower and supported me in going

beyond the typical compliance role in a way that had a real impact on struggling borrowers," she stated (Lux 2018).

In 2017, Mayotte left ASA to form a new nonprofit organization called The Institute of Student Loan Advisors (TISLA). She made this decision because ASA shifted its energies toward the broader goal of higher education attainment, "and while I appreciated the new mission, I realized that I had the opportunity to impact more people in a positive way by sticking with the student loan repayment area," she explained. "It's what I'm good at, and with 44 million student loan borrowers out there and almost a third of them struggling with their debts, there's a lot of people that need help" (Lux 2018).

TISLA's main focus involved counseling student borrowers about their best loan options and the most sensible approaches for paying off the debts they accrue for college. Under Mayotte's leadership, the organization also emerged as a leading critic of unscrupulous for-profit colleges and "debt relief" companies that prey on financially vulnerable students. TISLA maintained its operations by offering loan information services to professional societies and large employers, as well as by receiving grants and other financial assistance from philanthropic foundations.

According to Mayotte, people need her services and expertise because America's student loan programs are exceptionally difficult to navigate and full of financial dangers—especially since the Donald Trump administration rolled back reforms passed under the Barack Obama administration designed to better protect student borrowers. "The [student loan] programs are more complicated than they need to be," she said. As an example, she added, "There's two plans called income-based repayment, or IBR, and they're both different from each other. One of them takes 10 percent of your discretionary income. The other one takes 15. One forgives in 20 years, the other forgives in 25. You know, how would anybody who didn't do this for a living for 20 years know that—they shouldn't be expected to" (Sale 2019).

Mayotte noted that many of the borrowers who approach TISLA for help feel cornered and hopeless. "They're either overwhelmed by their debt or they're overwhelmed by all the different options or the rules associated with them," she explained. "Some of them have an air of desperation. Some of them have some strong undertones of anger. I would even go so far as to use the word rage because they're so frustrated with their situation. The vast majority of them are people that are just looking for help" (Sale 2019). For many college graduates, student loan debt created a financial burden that prevented them from taking vacations, buying homes, starting families, saving for retirement, or achieving other goals.

Mayotte's work with TISLA made her one of the more visible advocates for student loan borrowers in the United States—as well as one of the nation's leading voices calling for reforms to America's student loan programs and meaningful regulation of the country's for-profit colleges. A former contributor to *U.S. News and World Report*'s Student Loan Ranger blog, she also served as a resource for journalists and scholars interested in gaining a greater understanding of the complex and often confusing world of student loans.

Further Reading

Lux, Michael. 2018. "Ask an Expert: Betsy Mayotte of the Institute of Student Loan Advisors." *Student Loan Sherpa,* January 18, 2018. https://studentloansherpa.com/expert-betsy-mayotte-institute-student-loan-advisors/.

Mayotte, Betsy. 2017. "Regs Needed to Protect Students from Bad Actors in Education." *The Hill,* March 22, 2017. https://thehill.com/opinion/letters/325304-regs-needed-to-protect-students-from-bad-actors-in-education.

Mayotte, Betsy. 2017. "Wise Ways to Choose a Student Loan Repayment Plan." *U.S. News and World Report,* Student Loan Ranger blog, July 12, 2017. https://www.usnews.com/education/blogs/student-loan-ranger/articles/2017-07-12/wise-ways-to-choose-a-student-loan-repayment-plan.

Sale, Anna. 2019. "The Student Loan Nerd Helping Borrowers One Email at a Time." *Death, Sex & Money* [podcast]. October 2, 2019. https://www.wnycstudios.org/podcasts/deathsexmoney/episodes/betsy-mayotte-student-loan-death-sex-money#ember12037087.

Elizabeth Warren (1949–)

U.S. senator who promoted tuition-free public college and student debt forgiveness

Elizabeth Ann Warren was born on June 22, 1949, in Oklahoma City, Oklahoma. She was the youngest of four children born to Pauline and Donald Herring. Warren's family often struggled to make ends meet, especially after her father suffered a debilitating heart attack when Warren was 12 years old. Warren began working at a young age to help her family cover medical bills and pay the mortgage.

A state champion debater in high school, Warren received a scholarship at age 16 to attend George Washington University. She dropped out of college in 1968 to marry her first husband, James Warren. The marriage produced two children, Amelia and Alexander. Warren returned to school at the University of Houston and completed a bachelor of science degree in speech pathology in 1970. She then spent a year working as a special education teacher at a public school. In 1972, Warren enrolled at Rutgers Law School in New Jersey. She earned her law degree and passed the bar examination in 1976. After her first marriage ended in divorce in 1978, Warren married law professor Bruce Mann in 1980.

Warren taught law for 30 years at such institutions as the University of Houston, Rutgers University, the University of Texas, the University of Pennsylvania, and Harvard University. She specialized in bankruptcy law and conducted groundbreaking research about its economic impact on middle-class consumers and working-class families. Much of Warren's scholarly work focused on large banks and other financial institutions. She found that these companies disproportionately targeted people of lower economic status, particularly people of color, and convinced them to sign up for credit cards, mortgages, student loans, and other debt instruments that ultimately led to their financial ruin.

Beginning in 1995, Warren advocated for improved bankruptcy laws as part of the congressional National Bankruptcy Review Commission. She also served as a member of the FDIC Advisory Committee on Economic Inclusion. During the recession that began in 2007, Warren felt that the federal government prioritized the financial interests of Wall Street banks over those of American citizens. She worked to help ordinary people by overseeing the implementation of the Emergency Economic Stabilization Act and the Troubled Asset Relief Program. In 2010, Warren played a leading role in forming the Consumer Financial Protection Bureau (CFPB), an organization that fights to protect families from fraudulent practices by credit card companies and other large financial institutions.

The CFPB encountered opposition from the banks, credit card companies, and mortgage firms whose business practices came under its scrutiny. Warren also came under criticism from Republican lawmakers who saw the CFPB as an example of government overreach. Yet she insisted that the CFPB played a vital role in protecting American consumers from powerful corporate interests, noting that it "returned more than $12 billion to American consumers who've been tricked by big banks and corporations" in the decade after its creation ("Meet Elizabeth Warren" 2020).

Warren initially hoped to be named director of the CFPB, but Republican opposition caused President Barack Obama to appoint Richard Cordray to the position instead. Following this disappointment, Warren set her sights on running for political office as a way to continue representing the interests of everyday Americans. In 2012, she successfully campaigned as a Democrat for a seat in the U.S. Senate. Upon taking the oath of office on January 3, 2013, Warren became the first female senator from

Massachusetts. In 2018, she was elected to a second term in Congress, where she continued to advocate for the rights of consumers in their dealings with powerful business interests.

As a former professor, Warren took particular interest in issues surrounding college affordability and student debt. She noted that skyrocketing tuition costs forced more and more students to borrow money to afford higher education. As student debt levels increased, however, wages remained stagnant, which left millions of Americans struggling for decades to pay off education loans. Warren placed much of the blame for the student debt crisis on the financial services industry, which used its political influence to strip most standard consumer protections from education loans. She pointed out, for instance, that student loans were the only type of debt that could not be discharged through bankruptcy. "The bankruptcy laws were written ... to give this extraordinary protection to the student loan agencies," she stated. "A special law just for those who make student loans. Credit card companies don't get that kind of protection despite all their lobbying. Home mortgage lenders don't get that kind of protection" (Schorn 2006).

Warren also noted that the federal government guaranteed student loans, meaning that lenders got repaid even if borrowers defaulted. In fact, between interest, penalties, and collection fees, some lenders generated more revenue from loans in default than from loans repaid in full. "How do you lose in a game like that? It's a great business model. I win from here; I win from there," Warren said. "It's a market in which the protection goes to the lender. And the students get served up like turkeys at the Thanksgiving dinner" (Schorn 2006). For some borrowers, all the penalties and fees inflated their loan balances to double or triple the original amount. Facing insurmountable and inescapable debt, many young people found it impossible to achieve such financial goals as purchasing homes, starting families, taking vacations, or saving for retirement.

In 2019, Warren announced her candidacy for the 2020 Democratic presidential nomination. She released a detailed platform of progressive policies to address the most pressing issues facing the country, from health care and immigration to income inequality and climate change. "It won't be enough to just undo the terrible acts of this administration," she said of President Donald Trump. "We can't afford to just tinker around the edges—a tax credit here, a regulation there. Our fight is for big, structural change. This is the fight of our lives. The fight to build an America where dreams are possible, an America that works for everyone" (Lee and Krieg 2019).

In the realm of higher education, Warren proposed making public college tuition-free for all Americans. She also promised to alleviate the student debt crisis by immediately canceling up to $50,000 in federal loans for 42 million Americans. Warren argued that student loan forgiveness, which she planned to accomplish through executive order, would "provide an enormous middle-class stimulus that will boost economic growth, increase home purchases, and fuel a new wave of small business formation" ("Affordable Higher Education for All" 2020).

After performing well in early polls, Warren dropped out of the presidential race in March 2020, during the Democratic primaries. She maintained her seat in the senate and ranked among the most influential progressive voices on the national stage. Widely considered to be a smart, detail-oriented, committed, and effective lawmaker, Warren also appeared on the short list of vice presidential candidates for the apparent Democratic nominee, Joe Biden. Warren authored more than ten books, including her best-selling 2014 autobiography *A Fighting Chance*. Summing up her political goals, Warren wrote, "I'm here to fight for something that I believe is worth absolutely everything: to give each one of our kids a fighting chance to build a future full of promise and discovery" (Warren 2014).

Further Reading

"Affordable Higher Education for All." 2020. https://elizabethwarren.com/plans/affordable-higher-education.

Lee, M.J., and Gregory Krieg. 2019. "Elizabeth Warren Kicks Off Presidential Campaign with Challenge to Super-Wealthy—and Other Democrats." CNN, February 9, 2019. https://www.cnn.com/2019/02/09/politics/elizabeth-warren-campaign-kickoff-massachusetts/index.html.

"Meet Elizabeth Warren." 2020. https://elizabethwarren.com/meet-elizabeth.

Nilsen, Ella. 2020. "Elizabeth Warren's Ambitious Plan to Bypass Congress and Erase Student Debt, Explained." Vox, January 16, 2020. https://www.vox.com/2020/1/16/21065338/elizabeth-warren-plan-to-erase-student-debt-explained.

Schorn, Daniel. 2006. "Sallie Mae's Success Too Costly?" *60 Minutes*, CBS News, May 5, 2006. https://www.cbsnews.com/news/sallie-maes-success-too-costly/5/.

Stewart, Emily. 2019. "Elizabeth Warren Has Just One Plan." Vox, September 20, 2019. https://www.vox.com/policy-and-politics/2019/9/20/20867899/elizabeth-warren-cfpb-founding-plans-obama-president.

Warren, Elizabeth. 2014. *A Fighting Chance*. New York: Holt.

Further Resources

College Affordability

Andrews, Michelle. 2018. "For Many College Students, Hunger Makes It 'Hard to Focus.'" NPR, July 31, 2018. https://www.npr.org/sections/health-shots/2018/07/31/634052183/for-many-college-students-hunger-makes-it-hard-to-focus.

Angulo, A. J. 2016. *Diploma Mills: How For-Profit Colleges Stiffed Students, Taxpayers, and the American Dream.* Baltimore: Johns Hopkins University Press.

Archibald, Robert B., and David H. Feldman. 2014. *Why Does College Cost So Much?* New York and London: Oxford University Press.

Barboy, Dante. 2019. "What It Looks Like to Be Hungry in College." Center for American Progress, December 19, 2019. https://www.americanprogress.org/issues/education-postsecondary/news/2019/12/19/478916/looks-like-hungry-college/.

Bartlett, Donald L., and James B. Steele. 2012. *The Betrayal of the American Dream.* New York: Public Affairs.

Bendix, Aria. 2017. "A Striking Number of College Students Are Hungry and Homeless." *Atlantic,* March 15, 2017. https://www.theatlantic.com/education/archive/2017/03/a-striking-number-of-college-students-are-hungry-and-homeless/519678/.

Bennett, William J. 1987. "Our Greedy Colleges." *New York Times,* February 18, 1987. https://www.nytimes.com/1987/02/18/opinion/our-greedy-colleges.html.

Blake, John. 2019. "The College Admissions Scam Opens a New Front in the Affirmative Action Debate." CNN, March 17, 2019. https://www.cnn.com/2019/03/17/us/college-cheating-scandal-affirmative-action-debate/index.html.

Bovard, James. 2018. "Starvation Problem in Universities? The Real College Problem Is Obesity." *USA Today,* April 11, 2018. https://www.usatoday.com/story/opinion/2018/04/11/obesity-not-starvation-real-problem-universities-column/500855002/.

Campos, Paul F. 2015. "The Real Reason College Tuition Costs So Much." *New York Times,* April 4, 2015. https://www.nytimes.com/2015/04/05/opinion/sunday/the-real-reason-college-tuition-costs-so-much.html.

Caplan, Bryan. 2018. *The Case against Education: Why the Education System Is a Waste of Time and Money.* Princeton, NJ: Princeton University Press.

Caplan, Bryan. 2018. "The World Might Be Better off without College for Everyone." *Atlantic,* January/February 2018. https://www.theatlantic.com/magazine/archive/2018/01/whats-college-good-for/546590/.

Clotfelter, Charles T. 2019. *Big-Time Sports in American Universities.* 2nd ed. Cambridge, UK: Cambridge University Press.

Collins, Randall. 2019. *The Credential Society: A Historical Sociology of Education and Stratification.* Legacy Edition. New York: Columbia University Press.

Craig, Ryan. 2015. *College Disrupted: The Great Unbundling of Higher Education.* New York: St. Martin's Press.

Craig, Ryan. 2019. "Technology 1, 'Credential Society' 0." *Inside Higher Ed,* July 24, 2019. https://www.insidehighered.com/digital-learning/views/2019/07/24/1979-book-arguing-education-about-credentialing-not-skills-rings.

Davidson, Adam. 2015. "Is College Tuition Really Too High?" *New York Times Magazine,* September 13, 2015. https://www.nytimes.com/2015/09/13/magazine/is-college-tuition-too-high.html?_r=1.

Deruy, Emily. 2017. "Measuring College (Un)Affordability." *Atlantic,* March 23, 2017. https://www.theatlantic.com/education/archive/2017/03/measuring-college-unaffordability/520476/.

Duggan, Cherone. 2020. "Could College Be Free?" *Harvard Magazine,* January-February 2020. https://harvardmagazine.com/2020/01/free-college-deming.

Flannery, Mary Ellen. 2018. "Despite Widespread Fraud, For-Profit Colleges Get Green Light from DeVos." *NEA Today,* June 1, 2018. http://neatoday.org/2018/06/01/for-profit-colleges-fraud/.

Friedersdorf, Conor. 2013. "Universal Free College Would Be a Regressive Scandal." *Atlantic,* July 30, 2013. https://www.theatlantic.com/politics/archive/2013/07/universal-free-college-would-be-a-regressive-scandal/278201/.

Fry, Richard, and Anthony Cilluffo. 2019. "A Rising Share of Undergraduate Students Are from Poor Families, Especially at Less Selective Colleges." Pew Research Center, May 22, 2019. https://www.pewsocialtrends.org/2019/05/22/a-rising-share-of-undergraduates-are-from-poor-families-especially-at-less-selective-colleges/.

Gaul, Gilbert M. 2015. *Billion-Dollar Ball: A Journey Through the Big-Money Culture of College Football.* New York: Penguin.

Geiger, Roger L. 2015. *The History of American Higher Education.* Princeton, NJ: Princeton University Press.

Golden, Daniel. 2006. *The Price of Admission: How America's Ruling Class Buys Its Way into Elite Colleges—And Who Gets Left Outside the Gates.* New York: Random House.

Golden, Daniel, and Doris Burke. 2019. "The Unseen Student Victims of the 'Varsity Blues' College Admissions Scandal." *The New Yorker,* October 8, 2019. https://www.newyorker.com/books/page-turner/the-unseen-student-victims-of-the-varsity-blues-college-admissions-scandal.

Goldrick-Rab, Sara, Jed Richardson, Joel Schneider, Anthony Hernandez, and Clare Cady. 2018. "Still Hungry and Homeless in College." Wisconsin HOPE Lab, April 2018. https://hope4college.com/wp-content/uploads/2018/09/Wisconsin-HOPE-Lab-Still-Hungry-and-Homeless.pdf.

Goldrick-Rab, Sara, Robert Kelchen, Douglas N. Harris, and James Benson. 2016. "Reducing Income Inequality in Educational Attainment: Experimental Evidence on the Impact of Financial Aid on College Completion." *American Journal of Sociology 121*(6): 1762–1817. https://hope4college.com/wp-content/uploads/2018/09/Goldrick-Rab-etal-Reducing-Income-Inequality-in-Educational-Attainment.pdf.

Green, Douglas. 2019. "Why Has the Cost of College Outpaced Inflation?" *Education Week Teacher,* April 18, 2019. http://blogs.edweek.org/teachers/work_in_progress/2019/04/why_has_the_cost_of_college_ou.html.

Harris, Adam. 2019. "Millions of College Students Are Going Hungry." *Atlantic,* January 9, 2019. https://www.theatlantic.com/education/archive/2019/01/college-student-hunger/579877/.

Health, Education, Labor, and Pensions (HELP) Committee. 2012. "For-Profit Higher Education: The Failure to Safeguard the Federal Investment and Ensure Student Success." U.S. Senate, July 30, 2012. https://www.help.senate.gov/imo/media/for_profit_report/PartI-PartIII-SelectedAppendixes.pdf.

Hill, Catherine B. 2013. "Higher Education's Biggest Challenge Is Income Inequality." *Washington Post,* September 6, 2013. https://www.washingtonpost.com/opinions/higher-educations-biggest-challenge-is-income-inequality/2013/09/06/94b809a8-15ac-11e3-be6e-dc6ae8a5b3a8_story.html.

Holt, Alexander. 2015. "How One University President Is Trying to Save Public Higher Ed." *Atlantic,* September 23, 2015. https://www.theatlantic.com/education/archive/2015/09/lsu-debt-free-college/406555/.

Johnson, Daniel M. 2018. *The Uncertain Future of American Higher Education: Student-Centered Strategies for Sustainability.* London: Palgrave Macmillan.

Kahlenberg, Richard D. 2019. *Restoring the American Dream: Providing Community Colleges with the Resources They Need.* Washington, DC: Brookings Institution.

Kirkland, Justin. 2019. "The Lori Loughlin and Felicity Huffman College Admissions Scam Is So Much Bigger Than Two Celebrities." *Esquire,* March 12, 2019. https://www.esquire.com/entertainment/a26800556/operation-varsity-blues-explainer/.

Labaree, David F. 1997. *How to Succeed in School without Really Learning: The Credentials Race in American Education.* New Haven, CT: Yale University Press.

Labaree, David F. 2017. *A Perfect Mess: The Unlikely Ascendancy of Higher Education.* Chicago and London: University of Chicago Press.

Laterman, Kaya. 2019. "Tuition or Dinner? Nearly Half of College Students Surveyed in a New Report Are Going Hungry." *New York Times,* May 2, 2019. https://www.nytimes.com/2019/05/02/nyregion/hunger-college-food-insecurity.html.

Lederman, Doug. 2017. "Is Higher Education Really Losing the Public?" *Inside Higher Ed,* December 15, 2017. https://www.insidehighered.com/news/2017/12/15/public-really-losing-faith-higher-education.

Leef, George. 2020. "How College Sports Turned into a Corrupt Mega-Business." James G. Martin Center for Academic Renewal. March 11, 2020. https://www.jamesgmartin.center/2020/03/how-college-sports-turned-into-a-corrupt-mega-business/.

Maldonado, Camilo. 2018. "Price of College Increasing Almost 8 Times Faster Than Wages." *Forbes,* July 24, 2018. https://www.forbes.com/sites/camilomaldonado/2018/07/24/price-of-college-increasing-almost-8-times-faster-than-wages/#7ea381c66c1d.

Marcus, Jon, and Holly K. Hacker. 2015. "The Rich-Poor Divide on America's College Campuses Is Getting Wider, Fast." Hechinger Report, December 17, 2015. https://hechingerreport.org/the-socioeconomic-divide-on-americas-college-campuses-is-getting-wider-fast/.

Marcus, Jon. 2017. "In an Era of Inequity, More and More College Financial Aid Is Going to the Rich." Hechinger Report, December 7, 2017. https://hechingerreport.org/era-inequity-college-financial-aid-going-rich/.

Martin, Emmie. 2017. "Here's How Much More Expensive It Is for You to Go to College Than It Was for Your Parents." CNBC, November 29, 2017. https://www.cnbc.com/2017/11/29/how-much-college-tuition-has-increased-from-1988-to-2018.html.

Mathewson, Tara García. 2017. "A Tough-to-Swallow Reason College Keeps Costing More: The Price of Meal Plans." Hechinger Report, January 18, 2017. https://hechingerreport.org/tough-swallow-reason-college-keeps-costing-price-meal-plans/.

McMillan Cottom, Tressie. 2018. *Lower Ed: The Troubling Rise of For-Profit Colleges in the New Economy.* New York: New Press.

Mettler, Suzanne. 2014. *Degrees of Inequality: How the Politics of Higher Education Sabotaged the American Dream.* New York: Basic Books.

Mintz, Steven. 2017. "Eleven Lessons from the History of Higher Ed." *Inside Higher Ed,* May 7, 2017. https://www.insidehighered.com/blogs/higher-ed-gamma/11-lessons-history-higher-ed.

Mulhere, Kaitlin. 2018. "A Growing Number of States Are Spending Less on Public College Students." *Money,* March 29, 2018. https://money.com/state-public-college-funding-cuts-2017/.

Nadworny, Elissa, and Clare Lombardo. 2019. "Report: College Students Are Hungry and Government Programs Could Do More to Help." NPR, January 10, 2019. https://www.npr.org/2019/01/10/683302685/report-college-students-are-hungry-and-government-programs-could-do-more-to-help.

Neem, Johann N. 2019. *What's the Point of College? Seeking Purpose in an Age of Reform.* Baltimore: Johns Hopkins University Press.

Nevins, Jake. 2018. "'Phenomenally Saddening': Inside the Sordid World of America's For-Profit Colleges." *Guardian,* November 9, 2018. https://www.theguardian.com/film/2018/nov/09/fail-state-documentary-for-profit-colleges.

Newberry, Laura, and Hannah Fry. 2019. "The Legal Way the Rich Get Their Kids into Elite Colleges: Huge Donations for Years."*Los Angeles Times,* March 22, 2019. https://www.latimes.com/local/lanow/la-me-ln-college-admissions-scandal-legal-ways-20190318-story.html

Newfield, Christopher. 2016. *The Great Mistake: How We Wrecked Public Universities and How We Can Fix Them.* Baltimore: Johns Hopkins University Press.

Nilsen, Emma. 2019. "Progressives Want to Go Further Than Tuition-Free College—Here's Their Proposal to Make It Debt-Free." Vox, March 7, 2019. https://www.vox.com/2019/3/7/18252270/progressives-tuition-debt-free-college-schatz-pocan.

Otero-Amad, Farah. 2019. "Hunger on Campus: The Fight against Student Food Insecurity." NBC News, December 1, 2019. https://www.nbcnews.com/news/us-news/hunger-campus-fight-against-student-food-insecurity-n1063291.

Pallardy, Richard. 2019. "Are Lavish Facilities Responsible for Tuition Inflation?" SavingForCollege.com, May 16, 2019. https://www.savingforcollege.com/article/are-lavish-facilities-responsible-for-tuition-inflation.

Parker, Kim. 2019. "The Growing Partisan Divide in Views of Higher Education." Pew Research Center, August 19, 2019. https://www.pewsocialtrends.org/essay/the-growing-partisan-divide-in-views-of-higher-education/.

Pell Institute. 2019. "Indicators of Higher Education Equity in the United States: 2019 Historical Trend Report." http://pellinstitute.org/downloads/publications-Indicators_of_Higher_Education_Equity_in_the_US_2019_Historical_Trend_Report.pdf.

Pelletier, John. 2011. "Why Occupy Colleges?" *Inside Higher Ed,* October 7, 2011. https://www.insidehighered.com/views/2011/10/07/why-occupy-colleges.

Selingo, Jeffrey J. 2016. "The Biggest Problem Facing Higher Education, in One Chart." *Washington Post,* March 8, 2016. https://www.washingtonpost.com/news/grade-point/wp/2016/03/08/the-biggest-problem-facing-higher-education-in-one-chart/?noredirect=on.

Simon, Caroline. 2018. "For-Profit Colleges' Teachable Moment: 'Terrible Outcomes Are Very Profitable. *Forbes,* March 19, 2018. https://www. forbes.com/sites/schoolboard/2018/03/19/for-profit-colleges-teachable-moment-terrible-outcomes-are-very-profitable/#5f58805140f5.

Smith, Ashley A. 2019. "Poll: Voters Oppose Free College, Loan Forgiveness." *Inside Higher Ed,* May 1, 2019. https://www.insidehighered.com/quicktakes/2019/05/01/poll-voters-oppose-free-college-loan-forgiveness.

Stewart, Emily. 2019. "Elizabeth Warren Has Just One Plan." Vox, September 20, 2019. https://www.vox.com/policy-and-politics/2019/9/20/20867899/elizabeth-warren-cfpb-founding-plans-obama-president.

Strauss, Valerie. 2020. "There's a Lot of Talk about Changing College Admissions after the Varsity Blues Scandal—Don't Hold Your Breath." *Washington Post,* February 15, 2020. https://www.washingtonpost.com/education/2020/02/15/theres-lot-talk-about-changing-college-admissions-after-varsity-blues-scandal-dont-hold-your-breath/.

Taylor, Kelley. 2018. "College Affordability Guides Provoke Debate, Action on Economic Inequality on Campus." *Insight into Diversity,* October 18, 2018. https://www.insightintodiversity.com/college-affordability-guides-provoke-debate-action-on-economic-inequality-on-campuses/.

Thelin, John R. 2011. *A History of American Higher Education.* 2d Ed. Baltimore, MD: Johns Hopkins University Press.

Tough, Paul. 2019. *The Years That Matter Most: How College Makes or Breaks Us.* Boston: Houghton Mifflin.

Vedder, Richard. 2010. "The Great College-Degree Scam." *Chronicle of Higher Education,* December 9, 2010. https://www.chronicle.com/blogs/innovations/the-great-college-degree-scam/28067.

Verbruggen, Robert. 2019. "College Students Are Not Starving." *National Review,* May 3, 2019. https://www.nationalreview.com/corner/college-students-are-not-starving/.

Weissmann, Jordan. 2019. "Critics Complain That Free College Wouldn't Be Progressive. They're Missing the Point." Slate, May 6, 2019. https://slate.com/business/2019/05/free-college-tuition-warren-sanders.html.

Whistle, Wesley, and Tamara Hiler. 2019. "Why Free College Could Increase Inequality." Third Way, March 19, 2019. https://www.thirdway.org/memo/why-free-college-could-increase-inequality.

Willen, Liz. 2020. "After 'Varsity Blues' Scandal, Lots of Talk about Overhauling College Admissions. Will There Be Action?" *Hechinger Report,* February 4, 2020. https://hechingerreport.org/after-varsity-blues-scandal-lots-of-talk-about-overhauling-college-admissions-will-there-be-action/.

Yglesias, Matthew. 2019. "Democrats' Ongoing Argument about Free College, Explained." Vox, June 24, 2019. https://www.vox.com/2019/6/24/18677785/democrats-free-college-sanders-warren-biden.

Zinshteyn, Mikhail. 2016. "The Growing College-Degree Wealth Gap." *Atlantic,* April 25, 2016. https://www.theatlantic.com/education/archive/2016/04/the-growing-wealth-gap-in-who-earns-college-degrees/479688/.

Student Debt

Akers, Beth, and Matthew M. Chingos. 2018. *Game of Loans: The Rhetoric and Reality of Student Debt.* Princeton, NJ: Princeton University Press.

American Student Assistance. 2017. *Retirement Delayed: The Impact of Student Debt on the Daily Lives of Older Americans.* https://file.asa.org/wp-content/uploads/2018/08/14141828/retirement-delayed-2017-1.pdf.

Amselem, Mary Clare. 2019. "No, Your Student Loans Should Not Be Forgiven." Heritage Foundation, July 1, 2019. https://www.heritage.org/education/commentary/no-your-student-loans-should-not-be-forgiven.

Arnold, Chris. 2019. "Student Loans a Lot Like the Subprime Mortgage Debacle, Watchdog Says." NPR, December 9, 2019. https://www.npr.org/2019/12/09/785527874/student-loans-a-lot-like-the-subprime-mortgage-debacle-watchdog-says.

Associated Press. 2017. "For-Profit Colleges Linked to Almost All Loan Fraud Claims." CBS News, November 9, 2017. https://www.cbsnews.com/news/study-most-student-loan-fraud-claims-involve-for-profits/.

Associated Press. 2018. "Top U.S. Student Loans Official Resigns over 'Open Hostility' from White House." *Guardian,* August 27, 2018. https://www.theguardian.com/us-news/2018/aug/27/seth-frotman-student-loan-ombudsman-resigns-white-house-hostility.

Berman, Jillian. 2018. "America's $1.5 Trillion Student-Loan Industry Is a 'Failed Social Experiment.'" MarketWatch, October 18, 2018. https://www.marketwatch.com/story/americas-15-trillion-student-debt-is-a-failed-social-experiment-2018-10-16?mod=article_inline.

Brink Editorial Staff. 2019. "Is Student Debt Dragging Down the U.S. Economy?" Brink, August 22, 2019. https://www.brinknews.com/is-student-debt-dragging-down-the-u-s-economy/.

Carrns, Ann. 2019. "Two-Thirds of College Students Take on Debt, but Amount Is Rising More Slowly." *New York Times,* September 27 2019. https://www.nytimes.com/2019/09/27/your-money/student-debt-what-to-do.html.

Chinni, Dante, and Sally Bronston. 2019. "The Real College Crisis: Student Debt Drags Down Economy." NBC News, March 17, 2019. https://www.nbcnews.com/politics/meet-the-press/real-college-crisis-student-debt-drags-down-economy-n984131.

Cilluffo, Anthony. 2019. "Five Facts about Student Loans." Pew Research Center, August 13, 2019. https://www.pewresearch.org/fact-tank/2019/08/13/facts-about-student-loans/.

Collinge, Alan Michael. 2009. *The Student Loan Scam: The Most Oppressive Debt in U.S. History—and How We Can Fight Back.* Boston: Beacon Press, 2009.

Dickler, Jessica. 2017. "Student Loans Take a Mental Toll on Young People." CNBC, October 17, 2017. https://www.cnbc.com/2017/10/17/student-loans-take-a-mental-toll-on-young-people.html.

Farrington, Robert. 2018. "Why the Student Loan Bubble Won't Burst." *Forbes,* December 12, 2018. https://www.forbes.com/sites/robertfarrington/2018/12/12/student-loan-bubble-wont-burst/#594682156768.

Friedman, Zach. 2019. "Student Loan Debt Statistics in 2019: A $1.5 Trillion Crisis." *Forbes,* February 25, 2019. https://www.forbes.com/sites/zackfriedman/2019/02/25/student-loan-debt-statistics-2019/#3bb42199133f.

Friedman, Zack. 2020. "This Is What Happens If $1.6 Trillion of Student Loans Are Forgiven." *Forbes,* February 2, 2020. https://www.forbes.com/sites/zackfriedman/2020/02/02/student-loans-bernie-sanders-elizabeth-warren/#2f07e33035e1.

Girouard, John E. 2018. "How Student Debt Is Destroying the Economy and How We Can Stop It in Its Tracks." *Forbes,* November 8, 2018. https://www.forbes.com/sites/investor/2018/11/08/how-student-debt-is-destroying-the-economy-and-how-we-can-stop-it-in-its-tracks/#15f2fa796619.

Goldrick-Rab, Sara. 2016. *Paying the Price: College Costs, Financial Aid, and the Betrayal of the American Dream.* Chicago: University of Chicago Press.

Healey, Patrick B. 2019. "We Should All Be Concerned about the Student Debt Crisis." CNBC, November 4, 2019. https://www.cnbc.com/2019/11/04/we-should-all-be-concerned-about-the-student-debt-crisis.html.

Hembree, Diana. 2018. "New Report Finds Student Debt Burden Has 'Disastrous Domino Effect' on Millions of Americans." *Forbes,* November 1, 2018. https://www.forbes.com/sites/dianahembree/2018/11/01/new-report-finds-student-debt-burden-has-disastrous-domino-effect-on-millions-of-americans/#3953c90c12d1.

Hsu, Hua. 2019. "Student Debt Is Transforming the American Family." *New Yorker,* September 9, 2019. https://www.newyorker.com/magazine/2019/09/09/student-debt-is-transforming-the-american-family.

Ingraham, Christopher. 2019. "Seven Ways $1.6 Trillion in Student Loan Debt Affects the U.S. Economy." *Washington Post,* June 25, 2019. https://www.washingtonpost.com/business/2019/06/25/heres-what-trillion-student-loan-debt-is-doing-us-economy/.

Insler, Shannon. 2017. "The Mental Toll of Student Debt: What Our Survey Shows." Student Loan Hero, September 7, 2017. https://studentloanhero.com/featured/psychological-effects-of-debt-survey-results/.

Johnson, Daniel M. 2019. "What Will It Take to Solve the Student Loan Crisis?" *Harvard Business Review,* September 23, 2019. https://hbr.org/2019/09/what-will-it-take-to-solve-the-student-loan-crisis.

Keshner, Andrew. 2018. "How Student-Loan Debt Affects the Rest of Your Life (It's Not Pretty)." MarketWatch, November 20, 2018. https://www.marketwatch.com/story/what-student-debt-does-to-people-its-not-pretty-2018-11-14.

Kirsch, Daniel T. 2019. *Sold My Soul for a Student Loan: Higher Education and the Political Economy of the Future.* Santa Barbara, CA: Praeger.

Koch, James. V. 2019. *The Impoverishment of the American College Student.* Washington, DC: Brookings Institution.

Liebenthal, Ryann. 2018. "Unforgivable: The Incredible, Rage-Inducing Inside Story of America's Student Debt Machine." *Mother Jones,* September/

October 2018. https://www.motherjones.com/politics/2018/08/debt-student-loan-forgiveness-betsy-devos-education-department-fedloan/.

Livni, Ephrat. 2018. "$1.5 Trillion of Student Loan Debt Has Transformed the American Dream." Quartz, August 24, 2018. https://qz.com/1367412/1-5-trillion-of-us-student-loan-debt-has-transformed-the-american-dream/.

Looney, Adam. 2019. "How Progressive Is Senator Elizabeth Warren's Loan Forgiveness Proposal?" Brookings, April 24, 2019. https://www.brookings.edu/blog/up-front/2019/04/24/how-progressive-is-senator-elizabeth-warrens-loan-forgiveness-proposal/.

Looney, Adam, David Wessel, and Kadija Yilla. 2020. "Who Owes All That Student Debt? And Who'd Benefit If It Were Forgiven?" Brookings, January 28, 2020. https://www.brookings.edu/policy2020/votervital/who-owes-all-that-student-debt-and-whod-benefit-if-it-were-forgiven/.

Loonin, Deanne. 2014. "The Sallie Mae Saga: A Government-Created, Student-Debt Fueled Profit Machine." National Consumer Law Center, January 2014. https://www.studentloanborrowerassistance.org/wp-content/uploads/File/report-sallie-mae-saga.pdf.

MacLellan, Lila. 2019. "It's Time to Talk about the Mental Health Effects of Student Loan Debt." Quartz, October 28, 2019. https://qz.com/work/1732070/the-emotional-toll-of-student-loan-debt-at-work/.

McHarris, Philip V., and Zellie Imani. 2020. "It Is Time to Cancel Student Debt and Make Higher Education Free." *Al Jazeera,* April 26, 2020. https://www.aljazeera.com/indepth/opinion/time-cancel-student-debt-higher-education-free-200425104050766.html.

Murakami, Kery. 2020. "Is Canceling Student Debt the Right Approach?" *Inside Higher Ed,* April 1, 2020. https://www.insidehighered.com/news/2020/04/01/progressives-were-divided-over-widespread-cancellation-student-debt-stimulus.

Nadworny, Elissa, and Clare Lombardo. 2019. "'I'm Drowning': Those Hit Hardest by Student Loan Debt Never Finished College." NPR, July 18, 2019. https://www.npr.org/2019/07/18/739451168/i-m-drowning-those-hit-hardest-by-student-loan-debt-never-finished-college.

Nadworny, Elissa. 2019. "These Are the People Struggling the Most to Pay Back Student Loans." NPR, July 9, 2019. https://www.npr.org/2019/07/09/738985632/these-are-the-people-struggling-the-most-to-pay-back-student-loans.

Nova, Annie. 2018. "More Than One Million People Default on Their Student Loans Each Year." CNBC, August 13, 2018. https://www.cnbc.com/2018/08/13/twenty-two-percent-of-student-loan-borrowers-fall-into-default.html.

Ortiz, Erik. 2019. "Inside the Education Department's Effort to 'Obstruct' Student Loan Investigations." NBC News, September 9, 2019. https://www.nbcnews.com/news/education/inside-education-department-s-effort-obstruct-student-loan-investigations-n1049576?icid=related.

Schorn, Daniel. 2006. "Sallie Mae's Success Too Costly?" *60 Minutes,* CBS News, May 5, 2006. https://www.cbsnews.com/news/sallie-maes-success-too-costly/5/.

Swaminathan, Aarthi. 2020. "Trump Administration Plan to Sunset the Public Service Loan Forgiveness Program Would Be 'Devastating,' Expert Says." Yahoo! Finance, March 7, 2020. https://finance.yahoo.com/news/pslf-program-sunset-student-loans-135004757.html.

Taylor, Astra. 2020. "Cancelling Student Debt Was Always the Right Thing to Do. Now It's Imperative." *Guardian,* April 7, 2020. https://www.theguardian.com/commentisfree/2020/apr/07/cancel-student-debt-coronavirus.

Turner, Cory. 2018. "Why Public Service Loan Forgiveness Is So Unforgiving." NPR, October 17, 2018. https://www.npr.org/2018/10/17/653853227/the-student-loan-whistleblower.

Valenti, Joe, Sarah Edelman, and Tobin Van Ostern. 2013. "Student-Loan Debt Has a Rippling Negative Effect on the Broader Economy." American Progress, April 10, 2013. https://www.americanprogress.org/issues/higher-education/news/2013/04/10/60173/student-loan-debt-has-a-rippling-negative-effect-on-the-broader-economy/.

Verbruggen, Robert. 2019. "Myths of Student Loan Debt." *National Review,* July 11, 2019. https://www.nationalreview.com/magazine/2019/07/29/myths-of-student-loan-debt/?itm_source=parsely-api.

Zaloom, Caitlin. 2019. *Indebted: How Families Make College Work at Any Cost.* Princeton, NJ: Princeton University Press.

Resources for Students and Families Navigating College Costs and Debt

Consumer Financial Protection Bureau (CFPB). "Student Loans." https://www.consumerfinance.gov/consumer-tools/student-loans/.

"A Guide for College Students: How to Get a Degree Without Debt." Moneygeek. https://www.moneygeek.com/financial-planning/paying-for-college/resources/debt-free-college-education-guide/.

"Loans." CollegeBoard/BigFuture. https://bigfuture.collegeboard.org/pay-for-college/loans.

"Managing College Costs and Debt." Wharton School, University of Pennsylvania. https://kwhs.wharton.upenn.edu/kwhs-pwc-resources/managing-college-costs-and-debt/managing-college-costs-debt-full-podcast/.

"Paying for Education." 360 Degrees of Financial Literacy: American Institute of CPAs. https://www.360financialliteracy.org/Topics/Credit-and-Debt/Paying-for-Education.

Student Loan Justice. https://studentloanjustice.org/.

TISLA—The Institute for Student Loan Advisors. https://freestudentloanadvice.org/.

Index

Abernathy, Pauline, 45
Abrams, Natalie, 92
academic counseling, 63
accredited institutions, tax deductions for tuition paid to, 64
administrative costs, 23–24, 85
advanced coursework, 61
advanced degrees, pros and cons of, 17, 96, 113
aerospace engineering, 109, 110
affirmative action, 54
affluent students
    college enrollment for, 60
    college opportunities for, 4
    education costs, contribution to, 76
    financial assistance to, 56, 65
    free college plans slated to benefit, 78
    higher education access programs benefiting, 64
    high-performing schools, access to, 61
African Americans, 13, 15, 89–90
agriculture, higher education in, 13
Alexander, F. King (1963-), 2, 3, 101–104
American colonies, higher education in, 12
American Council of Education (ACE), 54
American Dream, 1, 61–62, 82–84, 85
American Opportunity Tax Credit, 64

American Revolution, 12
American Student Assistance, 90, 122–123
Amsalem, Mary Clare, 100
antiwar movement, 14, 15, 50, 112
Arrington, Doris, 60–61
associate's degrees, 14, 79
Association of American Universities, 13

baby-boom generation, 2, 14, 21
bachelor's degree completion, income disparities in, 5
bachelor's degree impact on earning power, 79
bachelor's degree recipients, racial disparity of, 89–90
bankruptcy law, 125, 126
bankruptcy protections, removal of, 29–30, 110
Baum, Sandra, 98
Bennett, William J., 15, 24
Bennett hypothesis, 24
Biden, Joe, 97, 127
black bachelor's degree recipients, default rate for, 84, 89–90, 96
black undergraduates, student loans by, 96
black voters, 15
"borrower defense" regulations, 44, 45
borrower education, 85

borrowers, student. *See* student
   borrowers
borrowing, growing reliance on, 95
Bovard, James, 73
Broton, Katharine, 70
Buckingham, Jack, 53
Bush, George W., 35
Buttigieg, Pete, 79

Calhoun, Mike, 84
California State University-Long
   Beach, 102
Campos, Paul F., 23
campus construction boom, rising
   tuition blamed on, 23
capitalist system, 85
Caplan, Bryan (1971-), 105–108
career paths, student debt impact on,
   82–83
CARES Act, 98
Carter, Jimmy, 15
Case against Education, The (Caplan), 106
Cellini, Stephanie, 42–43, 44
Century Foundation, 45
charter schools, 116, 117
Christian schools, 115, 116
cities going bankrupt, 77
civil rights movement, 14–15
class distinctions, 60, 63
Clinton, Bill, 1, 30
Clinton, Hillary, 111
Closing the College Hunger Gap Act, 73
co-educational institution, first, 13
Cold War, 14, 28
collection agencies, 110
college access, 18
college admissions consultants, 51–52,
   61
college admissions process, flaws
   in, 53–56
college admissions test preparation, 60
college affordability
   concerns over, 2
   and income inequality, 59–67

   issues surrounding, 126
   student aid and, 63–67
college affordability crisis
   credential inflation as factor in, 18
   economic inequality fueling, 67
college-building boom, 12
college completion issue, food
   insecurity as, 71
College Cost Reduction and Access Act
   (CCRAA), 35–36
college costs, lowering, proposals for, 85
college costs, skyrocketing, 2–4, 20–26,
   95, 126
college dropouts, 88
college education. *See* higher education
college enrollment, economic
   disparities beginning with, 60
college entry, delaying, 8
college finance system, calls for
   overhauling, 94
college graduates
   financial burden on, easing, 28
   student debt impact on, 7
   unemployment for, 49–50
   wage stagnation for, 95
college graduation rates, income impact
   on, 63
college rankings, 3, 56
college scams, debt cancellation
   proposed for victims of, 99
college spending as college cost factor, 3
college students, prospective, affordable
   alternatives for, 85
Collinge, Alan Michael (1970-), 28,
   109–111
Collins, Randall (1941-), 17–20,
   112–114
Commission on Higher Education, 14
communities, indebtedness of, 96–97
community colleges
   debt incurred by students at, 89
   default rates for attenders at, 89
   development of, 14
   low-income students at, 62, 63

nontraditional students at, 70
recession impact on, 62
starting out at, 8
tuition elimination proposed for, 76
two-year, 76, 77, 79
community service, 61
Conflict Sociology (Collins), 113
Connolly, Caroline, 52
consolidation loans, 29, 109–110
consumer debt, student loan and other
  debts compared, 5, 27, 49, 126
Consumer Financial Protection Bureau
  creation and overview of, 36–39, 125
  leadership, 119–121
  student loan office, 35
consumer purchasing power, student
  debt impact on, 7
consumer spending, student debt
  impact on, 95
Conway, Jack, 41
Corinthian Colleges, 42, 43, 44, 120
COVID-19 pandemic, 97
Craig, Ryan, 19
credential inflation, 17–19, 113, 114
Credential Society, The (Collins), 17–20,
  113
Cuomo, Andrew, 71

Dannenberg, Michael, 99
Dartmouth College, 12
Davidson, Adam, 16–17, 21–22,
  25–26, 56, 65, 66
"debt relief" companies, 123
degree completion rates, income impact
  on, 5, 62–63
Del Pilar, Wil, 51
Del Rosario, Reniel, 72
DeMello, Tim, 91
Democratic presidential candidates
  college affordability solutions
    proposed by, 8, 73
  debt-free public college proposed
    by, 103
  structural change advocated by, 126

student debt cancellation proposed
  by, 97
student debt solutions proposed
  by, 86, 127
Department of Education (DOE)
  creation of, 15
  financial aid tracked by, 65
  fines imposed by, 42
  for-profit education sector
    regulation role of, 44
  loan forgiveness applications rejected
    by, 34–35, 38
  loan forgiveness granted by, 96
  loan payment freeze proposed
    for, 98
  PSLF program inaction by, 37
  student aid disbursed by, 15, 43
DeVos, Betsy (1958-)
  biography, 115–118
  consumer responsibility cited by, 42
  for-profit school targeting criticized
    by, 45
  public service loan forgiveness
    program ending announced by, 39
  student loan data restricted
    by, 120–121
  student loan servicer protection
    measures enacted by, 38
DeVos, Richard "Dick," 115–116
DeVry University, 45, 62
digital age, educational credential
  relevance in, 19–20
direct-aid model, 102
Dodd-Frank Wall Street Reform and
  Consumer Protection Act, 2010,
  36, 119
Duke University, 12
Dynarski, Susan, 88, 89

earnings potential, 20, 79, 93
economic growth, 20, 95
economic prosperity, higher education
  as pathway to, 59
economic system overhaul, calls for, 85

economic theory, 106
educated workers, employability and
    productivity of, 19
educated workforce, economic growth
    promoted by, 1
education
    access, disparities in, 51
    affordability, reduced of, 21–22
    economic growth affected by, 20
    stratification of, 56, 61, 112
educational attainment, income-based
    disparities in, 66
educational inequality, 107–108
educational outcomes, 43, 62
Education and Employment (Collins),
    113
education funding, economic cost of
    inadequate, 66
education grants, 15. *See also* Pell Grant
education levels, United States and
    other countries compared, 22
education loans, government-
    subsidized, 3
Education Trust, 51, 56, 65
Ehrenberg, Ron, 60, 64
elite colleges
    admissions obstacles, 53–54
    admissions reforms proposed, 56
    affluent student attendance at, 60, 61
    buying admission to, 51–53
    low-income student attendance
        at, 61
Emergency Economic Stabilization
    Act, 125
employers, student debt repayment
    assistance offered by, 93–94
employment prospects, 7, 27, 47, 48,
    49, 85
engineering, 13, 14, 34
Equal Rights Amendment, 15
extracurricular activities, 61

faculty salaries, stagnation of, 24
Fail State (documentary film), 42

families, starting, 91–92, 109, 123, 126
family health crisis, student debt
    increase following, 93
Farbman, Jason, 48
Farrington, Robert, 83, 85
Federal Direct Loan Program, 30, 31, 32
Federal Family Education Loan (FEEL)
    program, 29, 32
federal government, higher education
    financing role of, 28
federal programs, pitfalls of, 90–91
federal-state partnership, 103–104
federal student aid
    for-profit college tuition paid
        through, 40–41
    increased availability of, 3
    persons eligible for, 43
    tuition increases *versus,* 24–25
FedLoan, 37
Fighting Chance, A (Warren), 127
financial aid to students. *See* student aid
financial insecurity, student debt
    contribution to, 87, 92
financial security, student debt impact
    on, 83, 95
financial service industry, 99, 126
"first dollar" programs, 76
first-generation college students
    college affordability struggles of, 70
    for-profit education company
        targeting of, 42
    higher education access for, 40,
        60–61
    spots reserved for, calls for, 56
first-time college students, free tuition
    proposed for, 76
flagship public universities, 60, 61
food expenditures, students and
    average Americans compared, 70
food insecurity, 5, 68–72, 73–74
food pantries, 71–72
foreign language programs, 14
for-profit colleges
    black students at, 89

crackdown on fraudulent, 43–46, 85, 118, 120
critics of unscrupulous, 123
debt incurred by students at, 88, 89
default rates for attenders at, 89
educational outcomes at, 43, 62
low-income students at, 62
scams, 40–46
student aid for, 40–41
transparency of, 104
tuition elimination not proposed for, 76
for-profit college sector, emergence of, 40
for-profit schools as businesses, 41, 89
401(k) contributions, loan payments as, 86, 93
four-year colleges
affluent student attendance of, 78
costs at, 63
free tuition impact, potential on, 79
transfer to, 14, 62
tuition elimination proposed for, 76
four-year degree, full-time work required to pay for, 2
free college proposals, 76–80, 97
free-market approach to higher education, 8, 107–108
free speech movement, 14, 112
Friedersdorf, Conor, 77
Frotman, Seth (1978?-), 35, 37, 38, 119–121
full-time employment hours required to pay for college, 2

"gainful employment" rule, 44, 45
game shows, 97
geopolitical events, sociological foundations of, 113
George Mason University (GMU), 105–106
Giannulli, Mossimo, 52
G.I. Bill, 14, 28
Gilded Age, 59

Girouard, John E., 82, 86
global business environment, 1
global financial crisis, 119
Golden, Daniel, 55
golden age of higher education, 13–15
Goldrick-Rab, Sara, 70, 71
Government Accounting Office (GAO), 69
graduate students, debt incurred by, 88
Green, Douglas, 24–25
gross national product (GNP), 83, 95–96
Guaranteed Student Loan program, 15

Hamilton, Laura, 60, 63
Harrington, Ashley, 99
Harris, Adam, 69
Harvard University, 12
Harvey, Joshua Christopher, 49–50
haves and have-nots, 61, 107–108
Hayes, Jahana, 72
health, student debt impact on, 92, 110
health and food insecurity, 71
higher education
access to, expanding, 17, 64
affordability, goal of, 28, 103
demand for, increasing, 3
government funding for, 3, 22, 103, 107–108
history of, 11–15
income-based disparities in, 60–63
increased pursuit of, 22–23
public trust in, rebuilding, 104
reforming, 7–8
social mobility through, 59
socioeconomic equalizing, 60, 96
socioeconomic value of, 1
stratification of, 56, 61, 112
success-failure dividing line, 74
and tech jobs, 18–20
transparency in, 104
United States and other countries compared, 11–12

value of, questioning, 7–8, 16–20,
    22, 33, 49, 84, 104, 106–107, 113
Higher Education Act (HEA), 1965
    Guaranteed Student Loan program
        established through, 15
    origin and overview, 1–2
    reauthorizations and amendments,
        29–30, 35, 59, 73, 102
    signing of, 28–29
    Title IV, 43
    Title IX, 15, 101
high-income students, free tuition
    impact, potential on, 79
high-performing schools, 61
Hillman, Nick, 54
Historically Black Colleges and
    Universities (HBCU), 13
homelessness, 76, 77
homeownership rate, student debt
    impact on, 83
home purchase, first, 83, 91–92, 109,
    123, 126
Hope Center for College, Community,
    and Justice, 69
House Financial Services Committee, 38
household debt, student loan and other
    debts compared, 81
household net worth, student debt
    impact on, 83
housing, 73, 74, 91
housing insecurity, 70, 73–74
Hoyler, Maureen, 62
Huffman, Felicity, 52–53
hunger, 69, 74, 76

immigrants, 77
immigration, 107
income
    merit-based aid criteria correlated
        to, 65
    scholarship criteria correlation
        to, 25–26
    student performance correlated
        to, 56

unequal access and outcomes based
    on, 4–5
income-based loan repayment options,
    86
income-based repayment (IBR), 6, 35,
    123
income/economic inequality
    and college affordability, 59–67
    factors contributing to, 21–22,
        66, 67
    free tuition impact, potential on, 79
    in higher education, 60–63, 96
    movements aimed at addressing, 48
    recession and, 47
    reducing, 85
    student protests against, 49
    tuition-free college as factor in
        increasing, 77
income insecurity, 96–97
inflation rate, college costs outpacing,
    18, 20–21
information technology pioneers, 19–20
infrastructure, crumbling, 77
in-state students, free tuition proposed
    for, 76
The Institute of Student Loan Advisors
    (TISLA), 123–124
Interaction Ritual Chains (Collins), 113
ITT Technical Institute, 44, 62, 89, 120
Ivy League, formation of, 12
Ivy League education, 107, 112

Janavs, Grant, 54
Jindal, Bobby, 102, 103
jobs, changing, 19
Jobs, Steve, 19–20
job selection, student debt impact on, 82
job signaling, 107
Johns Hopkins University, 12
Johnson, Daniel M., 6, 8
Johnson, Lyndon B., 1–2, 15, 28–29

Khan, Shamus, 48
Kim, Joshua, 107–108

King, Brayden, 49
Kirwan, Brit, 5
knowledge, creation of, 113
Kushner, Jared, 55

land-grant colleges, 13
Langevin, Adam, 54
learning disabilities, false claims
    of, 52
Lelling, Andrew, 52
liberal arts colleges, 12–13
libertarian ideas and policies, 108
life decisions, student debt impact on,
    83, 87, 91–92, 95
Lincoln, Abraham, 13
living expenses
    cost of, 73–74
    debt-free college proposals and, 76,
        77, 78
    as educational expenses, 71
    struggle to meet, 70
    student aid to cover, 72–73
Livni, Ephrat, 33
loan servicers, 92–93
Lombardi, John V., 102
Loonin, Deanne, 31–32
Loughlin, Lori, 52
Louisiana state funding for public
        universities, 104
Louisiana State University (LSU),
        102–103, 104
low-income single mothers, for-profit
        college targeting of, 42
low-income students
    affordability and access for, 73
    college access obstacles faced by,
        4–5, 65–66, 67
    college affordability struggles of, 70
    college aid to, 2, 15, 29, 34, 70
    college types attended by, 62
    debt burden and default among, 90
    debt forgiveness for, 98
    debt-free college for, 77
    degree completion by, 62–63, 67

education expense as barrier for, 60
for-profit college targeting of, 42–43
free college plan value, potential to,
        77, 78
free tuition, potential for, 76, 79
higher education access for, 40, 59
hunger and homelessness faced
        by, 76
Louisiana State University, struggle
        to afford, 103
opportunities limited for, 61–62
shift away from aid benefiting,
        64, 65
spots reserved for, calls for, 56

Margetta-Morgan, Julie, 88, 91
marginalized groups, higher education
        access for, 40
Massachusetts Bay Colony, 12
Mayotte, Betsy (1973?-), 122–124
meal plans, 70
medicine, study of, 13, 34
merit-based financial aid, 60, 65, 67
merit-based scholarships, 4, 25–26,
        55–56, 64
meritocracy, theory of, 17
Merrill, Toby, 46
Mettler, Suzanne, 66
middle-class lifestyle, 7, 14, 109
middle-class stimulus, student debt
        elimination as, 86, 127
middle-class students, 70, 98
military advancements, 14
military arts, 13
military servicemembers and families,
        consumer protection for, 120
millennial generation
    American dream feasibility
        questioned by, 85
    economic conditions faced by, 49
    education funds, sources of, 21
    first home purchase by, 83
    higher education, attitudes
        concerning, 7–8

life choices available to, 82
student debt crisis impact on, 7
work to pay for college, 2
Miller, Ben, 90
minorities, 54, 84
Mitchell, Ted, 54
money and privilege, college
    admissions based on, 53
Moore, Michael, 111
Morehouse College, 97
Morrill, Justin Smith, 13
Morrill Land Grant Colleges Act, 1862,
    13
mortgage, 83, 84
Mount Holyoke College,
    Massachusetts, 13
Mulvaney, Mick, 38, 120, 121
Murphy, Chris, 73
Murray, Patty, 72–73
Myth of the Rational Voter, The (Caplan),
    106

Nader, Ralph, 30, 111
Nassirian, Barmak, 41
National School Lunch Program, 72
national service program, proposed, 80
national university, proposed, 12
nation-states, formation of, 113
Navient Corporation, 32, 36–37, 120
Newsome, Kenneth, 93
"90-10" rule, 44, 45
noneducational expenses as college cost
    factor, 3, 23–24, 67
nonprofit educational institutions
    costs at, 64
    debt incurred by students at, 88
    educational outcomes at, 62
    statistics, 40
    tuition elimination proposed for, 76
nonprofit model of higher education,
    41
nonprofit sector career, 83
nontraditional students, 40, 70, 73, 90
Nordlinger, Jay, 117–118

Obama, Barack
    appointments by, 125
    consumer protection act signed by,
        36, 119
    education guidelines established by,
        117, 118
    for-profit college scam crackdown
        under, 41
    for-profit education regulatory
        measures by, 44, 45
    higher education affordability
        importance cited by, 8
    Occupy Wall Street movement,
        views on, 48
    student debt concern voiced by, 28
    student loan system reform by, 32
    tuition-free college proposal
        advanced by, 76
Oberlin College, 13
Ocasio-Cortez, Alexandria, 82, 85
occupational training, 40
occupations, college degrees required
    for, 15
Occupy Colleges movement, 47–50
Occupy movement, 97
Occupy Wall Street movement,
    47, 48, 50
older Americans, households headed
    by, 90
O'Neill, Barbara, 82, 83
online courses, 8, 44
online learning, 40, 85
on-the-job training, 19
Open Borders (Caplan), 106
"Operation Varsity Blues" college
    admissions scandal, 50–56
opportunity, college role in providing, 1
Oregon state funding for public
    universities, 104

Paid Off with Michael Torpey (game
    show), 97
parenting, 106
part-time faculty, 24

part-time jobs, 63, 82
part-time students, 78
Pelletier, John, 49, 50
Pell Grant
    college costs not covered by, 63–64
    colleges attended by recipients of, 61,
        62, 77
    coverage provided through, 4
    debates over, 79–80
    expansion of, 29, 35
    increase proposed to, 66
    origin of, 102
    students not qualifying for, 70
Pell Grant recipients, 5, 77, 90
Pence, Mike, 117
people of color, 42
people with low self-esteem, 42
Pérez, Angel, 65
Perna, Laura, 61–62
personal crisis, 93
personal income, annual, 81
per-student state funding, 22–23
Petraeus, Holly, 120, 121
PLUS loans, 29
Pocan, Mark, 77
police officer job, education
    requirements for, 17
political science program funding, 14
political system overhaul, calls for, 85
poor-performing schools, federal
    funding to, 45
postsecondary enrollment, rise in, 14
postsecondary students, funding
    to, 15
poverty, cycle of, 97
Price of Admission, The (Golden), 55
Princeton University, 12
private colleges
    budgets of, 68
    professor salaries at, 102
    transparency of, 104
    tuition elimination not proposed
        for, 76
private education loans, 98

private lenders, crackdown on
    unscrupulous, 85
private school advocates, 115–118
professor salaries, private and public
    universities compared, 102
profit motive *versus* student interests, 44
Project on Predatory Student Lending, 46
Promoting Real Opportunity, Success,
    and Prosperity through Education
    Reform (PROSPER) Act, 45
public college, free, 8, 97
public college revenue, 22
public schools, 116, 117, 118
public-service career, 83
public-service jobs, 34, 35–36
Public Service Loan Forgiveness (PSLF)
    program, 34–39, 86, 96, 97
public universities
    debt-free, 77
    debt incurred by students at, 88
    flagship, 60, 61
    free, 97
    high-income students at, 79
    low-income students at, 62, 63
    professor salaries at, 102
    state support for, 102, 104
    transparency of, 104
    tuition elimination proposed for, 76
purchasing power, 84

quality of life, 91
QuinStreet, 42

racial disparities in student burdens and
    default rates, 89–90, 96
racial segregation in education, 13
Reagan, Ronald, 15, 24, 28
recession, 2008
    community colleges impacted by, 62
    consumer protection measures in
        wake of, 119
    employment prospects and student
        debt in, 7, 22, 23
    higher education impacted by, 103

income inequality in wake of, 47
relief programs during, 125
state funding for higher education reduced after, 78
student loan forgiveness advocated following, 97
student loans following, 95
recession, risk factors for, 82
Reed, Conor Tomás, 50
Reeves, Richard, 65–66
Remondi, Jack, 36–37
retirement
    obstacles to saving for, 83, 90, 92, 109, 123, 126
    student debts lasting into, 91
Rhode Island, 12
Riddell, Mark, 52
Rolling Jubilee, 97
Ruiz, Roman, 61

Sallie Mae (Student Loan Marketing Association, SLMA)
    establishment of, 6, 27, 29
    predatory practices of, 109–110, 111
    as private enterprise, 28, 30–32
    reorganization of, 32
    request for debt assistance, response to, 93
    and student debt crisis, 27–33
Sallie Mae Bank, 32
Sanders, Bernie, 75, 76, 77, 85, 97, 103
Schatz, Brian, 77
Schmoke, Julian, Jr., 45
Scholastic Aptitude Test (SAT), 52
school choice, 116, 117, 118
science, study of, 13, 14
Sealy, Will, 92
segregated public facilities, 14
selective institutions, 51
Selfish Reasons to Have More Kids (Caplan), 106
seniors, student debt burden of, 91
September 11, 2001 terrorist attacks, 110

Servicemen's Readjustment Act, 1944, 14
sex discrimination, prohibition of, 15
Shebanow, Alex, 43
Singer, William "Rick," 51–52, 53–54
sit-in protests, 14
small businesses, starting, 82
Smith, Robert F., 97
social conflict theory, 113
social equality, 18
socialism, 85
socially isolated, 42
social mobility, 17–18, 59
social stratification, 21
socioeconomic background, 51, 61
socioeconomic equalizer, higher education system not serving as, 60, 96
sociologists, 17–20, 112–114
Sociology of Philosophies, The (Collins), 113
Soviet Union, 14, 28, 113
Special Olympics, 118
Stafford loan program, 15, 29, 35
Stanford University, 12
states
    buy-in as free college requirement, 77–78
    college freedom from control by, 12
    universities, support for, 3, 22, 102, 103, 104
status attainment (term), 17
Stockman, David, 28
stress, 91, 92
struggling students, approaches to help, 71–74
student aid
    and affordability, 63–67
    applying for, 60
    availability of, 3
    dependence on, 27
    as fundamental aspect of education system, 117
    living expenses and, 70, 72–73

reforms to, 118
tuition increases *versus,* 4, 24–25
unequal distribution of, 25–26
Student Aid and Fiscal Responsibility
    Act, 2010, 32
student body diversity, 67
Student Borrower Bill of Rights, 111
Student Borrower Protection
    Center, 121
student borrowers
    death, loan forgiveness in event of, 96
    debt impact on, 84, 91–94, 95,
        109–111
    default among *see* (student loan
        default)
    protection measures, 38, 118, 120,
        123
    rights advocates, 122–124
student debt
    balance, 7, 27, 82, 88–91
    borrowers' lives impacted by, 91–94,
        95, 109–111, 123
    canceling, calls for, 39, 86
    college degree value *versus* high, 22
    economic impact of, 7, 33, 81–86
    factors contributing to, 78, 126
    federal programs aimed at
        alleviating, 90–91
    at for-profit schools, 62
    growing, 5–7, 95
    interest on, 27
    non-graduation combined with, 63
    repayment, 7, 88–91, 93–94
    total outstanding, 87
student debt crisis
    causes of, 29
    emergence of, 44
    federal government handling
        of, 38, 121
    financial services industry role
        in, 126
    identification of, 82
    impact of, 32–33
    organizations combating, 111

potential for new, 99–100
preventing, 96
resolving, proposals for, 85–86, 94,
    111, 127
Sallie Mae and, 27–33
student protests in face of, 49–50
Student Debt Crisis (organization), 91,
    92, 93
Student Debt Emergency Relief Act, 98
student debt forgiveness. *See also* Public
    Service Loan Forgiveness (PSLF)
    program
    applications, rejection of, 34–35
    in cases of fraud, 41, 44, 45
    as college affordability solution, 8
    objections to, 96, 98–100
    proposals for, 33, 39, 48, 86, 94,
        95–100, 127
student debt relief
    obstacles to obtaining, 37, 123
    options for, 6
    proposals for, 33, 86, 96–98
    for public service, 35–36
student demographic, for-profit college
    targeting of, 43, 89
student enrollment as source of profit,
    41–42
student-led social activism, 14–15,
    47–50, 111
student loan default
    among college dropouts, 88
    among for-profit school attendees, 44
    federal programs aimed at
        alleviating, 90–91
    impact of, 6, 27, 84–85, 110
    lender profits from, 30, 126
    provisions for potential, 29
    statistics, 6, 27, 41, 84, 88, 89, 90
student loan industry, 28–30, 111
StudentLoanJustice.org, 111
student loan programs, establishment
    of, 15
Student Loan Ranger blog, 124
student loan reform, 32–33, 111

student loans
    cancellation of, 44
    credential inflation *versus,* 18
    DeVos, B., record on, 118
    as fundamental aspect of education
        system, 117
    interest on, lowering, 86
    risks and benefits of, 31
    statistics, 21
    subsidized, 102
Student Loan Scam, The (Collinge), 28,
    111
Student Nonviolent Coordinating
    Committee, 14–15
student performance criteria, 56
student protests, 48–50
student role in higher education reform,
    8, 111
student room and board costs, 70, 76
students, negotiation with prospective, 25
Students for a Democratic Society, 15
students of color, 40, 96
students with disabilities, 40, 117
subprime mortgage housing bubble, 84
suicide, 92
Supplemental Nutrition Assistance
    Program (SNAP), 72
support services, 63
Swipe Out Hunger program, 72

Talwani, Indira, 52–53
tax breaks, 64
tax credits and deductions, 86
teacher-student interaction in online
    courses, 44
tech jobs, 18–20
technical skills, acquiring, 19
technical training, 66
technology, 13, 18–19
Temporary Expanded Public Service
    Loan Forgiveness Program
    (TEPSLF), 37–38
test-preparation services, 61
Title IV of Higher Education Act, 43

Title IX of Higher Education Act, 15, 101
Tobin, Morrie, 51
Torpey, Mike, 97
total permanent disability, loan
    forgiveness in event of, 96
Tough, Paul, 55–56
Transylvania University, 12
Trellis Company, 71
Troubled Asset Relief Program, 125
Truman, Harry S., 14
Trump, Donald
    appointments, 116–117
    criticism of, 35, 126
    relatives and family members, 55
    student borrower protection
        measures rolled back by, 41, 44,
        120, 123
Trump University, 41, 44
tuition costs, rising
    factors contributing to, 18, 23–24
    impact of, 2, 15, 87, 107
    prediction of, 102
    state disinvestment as factor in, 78
    state funding *versus,* 22, 103
    student aid *versus,* 4, 24–25
    student protests against, 49
tuition discounting, 4, 25–26
tuition-free college proposals, 8, 75–80
two-year community colleges, 76, 77, 79

underclass, 5
undergraduate students, debt incurred
    by, 88
undergraduate students in poverty, 62
underperforming schools, 60
unemployment, 49–50, 110
universities, war effort contributions
    by, 14
University of California-Berkeley,
    71–72
University of California-Los Angeles, 72
University of Phoenix, 62
upper-income students, 98
upward mobility, 16

Urban Institute, 78, 83, 98
U.S. economy
  limiting damage to, 84–86
  stimulating, 95–96
  student debt impact on, 7, 33, 81–86
U.S. gross national product (GNP), 83, 95–96
U.S. Senate Committee on Health, Education, Labor, and Pensions (HELP), 42, 43, 44
U.S. Supreme Court, 12

Vanderbilt University, 12
veterans
  consumer protection for, 120
  education benefits for, 14, 28, 34
  for-profit college scams aimed at, 42
Vietnam War, opposition to, 15, 50, 120
Violence (Collins), 113
vocational education, 66, 108

wage stagnation, 95, 126
Warren, Elizabeth (1949-)
  biography, 124–127
  college construction expenditures criticized by, 23
  as consumer protection advocate, 119
  debt-free public college proposed by, 103
  for-profit school regulation weakening criticized by, 45
  free college proposal by, 77, 78
  Sallie Mae criticized by, 31
  student debt forgiveness advocated by, 39, 86, 97, 98
Washington, George, 12
wealth and connections, college admissions based on, 53–54

wealth tax, 77, 97, 99
wealthy students
  advantages enjoyed by, 55, 61
  financial aid to, 60, 64, 65
  higher education favoring, 59–60
  scholarships to, 55–56, 64
  at selective colleges and universities, 5, 54, 61
websites, 111
Weissman, Jordan, 80, 118
western frontier, first college on, 12
white students at selective colleges and universities, 54
women
  equal educational and athletic opportunities for, 101
  for-profit education company targeting of, 42
  student debt burden impacting, 96
  student loan default by, 84
women's college, first, 13
women's movement, 14, 15
working adults, for-profit education company targeting of, 42
work-study opportunities, 15, 34, 64, 72
World War I (1914-1918), higher education during, 13–14
World War II (1939-1945), higher education during, 13–14

Years That Matter Most, The (Tough), 55–56
Yglesias, Matthew, 75, 77, 78, 80
young people from low-income families, higher education cost increase impact on, 21

Zaloom, Caitlin, 94

About the Author

Laurie Collier Hillstrom is a freelance writer and editor based in Brighton, Michigan. She is the author of more than 40 books in the areas of American history, biography, and current events. Her published works include four previous volumes in the 21st-Century Turning Points series—*The #MeToo Movement, School Shootings and the Never Again Movement, The Vaping Controversy,* and *Family Separation and the U.S.–Mexico Border Crisis*—as well as *Alexandria Ocasio-Cortez: A Biography* and *Defining Moments: The Constitution and the Bill of Rights.*